THE BLACK KNIGHTS

An Occult History of the Knights Templar and the English Covenant

Stephen J Ash

2007

Copyright Stephen J Ash 2007

This book is protected by a servitor,
all unattributed reproductions are
at your own considerable risk!

ISBN 978-1- 4092-1941- 5

Table of Contents

Acknowledgements

Introduction

Preface

Chapter 1 The Birth of the Templars	1
Chapter 2 The Hidden Roots of the Templars	23
Chapter 3 Templars Ascendant	43
Chapter 4 The Templars in England	59
Chapter 5 Pagan Precursors and the English Covenant	71
Chapter 6 The Heresies and Fall of the Templars	91
Chapter 7 Templar Survivals, Real and Imaginary	117
Conclusion	151

Ilustrations

Abraxas Seal	25
Temple and Dome of Rock	39
Persephone	116
London Pentagram	124

ACKNOWLEDGEMENTS

I would like to thank

Jen Barker, for invaluable assistance with the genealogies in this book and for constant support.

Geoff Gilbertson, for launching me on the research path.

Sean Scullion, for giving me the idea for the tourist walks that led to much of the research for this book.

Paul Devereux, for advice while researching the alignments.

David Barrett, for useful pointers and tough criticism.

My Ancestors and Patrons.

All those that have supported me during this journey.

Introduction

This is a book about a lost history, little of which has been seriously explored before. The reason for this I suggest is partly due to the way academic history is conventionally conceived and partly due to the poor popular writing that has been associated with this subject. History is a notoriously vague area of study, it has been said that with few exceptions there really is no true history, other than a fiction that the majority of historians agree on. I would concur with this but put it in more scientific terms. Given that historical evidence is conventionally taken to consist of contemporary documents, or some material 'footprint' left by an event, from which facts can be drawn, there simply is rarely enough of this evidence to support a clear picture of what actually occurred. The further back in time we go the more acute the problem becomes. In science this problem is known as the underdetermination of theory by evidence and is familiar to anyone who has been part of a research program of any kind. What usually happens in these circumstances is that a vast number of possible interpretations can be drawn, all of which fit the available evidence. So an arbitrary agreed criteria is normally chosen to decide between these. Common criteria for this are simplicity, which works well for physics, though perhaps a lot less well for history; rationality, a difficult criteria to apply to human relations; consistency, or how well the ideas fit with facts already established to be true, or with the consensus of what is considered the norm; and most subjectively of all, 'plausibility'. I would argue that all of these have deep flaws for the purpose of historical research. But worse still, due to the political and ideological importance of history expedient stories, drawn from the most conservative or diplomatic perspectives, are often adopted by historians seeking a comfortable life.

Another way to generate histories is just to be 'creative' and speculate widely and then criticize what we have to see if it stands up or not. If we are honest all too often it doesn't and we realise we've let our imagination run away from reality again, we've seen imaginary shapes in the inkblot. No matter how much we flatter our personal intuition it tends to let us down. Scholars know this and often tend to compensate with a more systematic scientific approach, though usually applied in the form of conservative overcompensation.
There is another better founded form of imagination however, that which I would call holistic intuition. This occurs when we see not just an imagined pattern in the data, but a recurring one, whose core components reinforce each other forming a broader overall pattern. One in which all inconsistencies have been eliminated.

When we do this, we no longer have to worry about 'well grounded evidence', as the strength of our history is found not in the reliability of its roots, but in the coherency of its elements. In their mutual support as a rhizomatic structure, rather than the usual hierarchy of facts. This is basically how human intuition functions. In doing this we also avail ourselves of far more evidence, including even casual rumour. All of which will be valuable if it fits into the greater whole and is supported by it. As long as we hang our more speculative flesh on a skeleton of fact, based on a broadly scientific method, this is an extremely powerful methodology and one adopted to great advantage in this book. The difficulty remains of presenting such a rhizomatic picture in the linear form of a book. To help this process the reader is asked not to view the thesis presented as a step by step argument, but rather as an emerging pattern from which a conclusion seems forced upon us.

The history thus proposed here occasionally veers from the sceptical position of academic orthodoxy. Yet it also rejects much of the airy fantasy that stretches credulity in this field. The book is presented as the current record of an ongoing research project. Some of the data may turn out to be coincidence and need winnowing out, but arguably there is too much for it all to be mere coincidence. Beyond this the reader is asked to view the story as a whole and ask themselves whether this history can be denied.

Preface

As a student of history and philosophy and a lover of all that is mysterious and arcane, I had long been intrigued by tales of the medieval Knights Templar, as well as other mysterious groups such as the Rosicrucians, the Bavarian Illuminati, the Sabbatic Witches and many more. Then while researching for the historical tours of London that I was developing at the time, I discovered a number of curious stories about the Templars, as well as some strange Geomantic alignments that also seemed to be traceable back to the mysterious Order. On closer examination of all this I unearthed a few curious facts regarding the unusual preoccupations of the Knights. Facts that would shed new light on their nature.

But it was only after researching my own family history, in a moment of curiosity, that I discovered one of my direct ancestors, John St Leger, was listed in church records in Devon as a 'Templar Master'. It was then that things began to get even more curious.

Strangely, records of such 'Templar knights' in Devon went up to the late 14th century, long after their official dissolution. What's more the St Leger family was related to a relatively small number of interrelated families in western England, some of whom had cropped up in my previous research. The actual branch of St Leger's I had unearthed turned out to be close supporters of the Marshall family in Ireland, arguably the real power behind the Templars in the 13th century, with whom they were in fact related via the de Clare family. As well as being relatives of the first English Templar Master Roger Hastings. This was certainly enough to cause me to investigate further.

Descended from a Saint and Burgundian advisor to the Neustrian Franks, St Leger family members went on to be Viceroys of Ireland and Jacobite Freemasons, amongst other distinctions. Revealing fascinating chains of family associations that would become central to my research. When the other related families were also investigated the same pattern tended to repeat itself. This genealogical study thus became the key to unlocking a hidden aspect of the Templars and discovering those I called the 'black knights'.

Sobered by the discovery that my family connection was extremely 'branched out', as genealogists like to put it - my nearest relatives by the 19th century being small scale farmers and horse trainers from Somerset, who later married into a Romany Gypsy family - I explored the broader lineages further. It seemed that while the Templar Order itself had died out a certain tradition appeared to have survived amongst certain branches of families descended from its senior members and supporters. A tradition that returned in many different forms over several generations.

At this stage many may have been tempted to fake an occult 'family tradition', as is the way in certain circles, especially given that several other branched out St Leger descendants were found in the Stuckley and Westcott families, to whom I was more closely related, many of whom had been associated with various fringe religious and Masonic societies, as well as quite a few Hermetic and Theosophical groups.[1] However nothing had found its way into my branch of this familial network, or at least nothing I can reveal at this time of course! But in all seriousness, I soon discovered that many of my friends with similar esoteric interests also had similar genealogies, often without realising it and I began to wonder if this was more widespread. Perhaps less about family traditions than about somekind of inheritance, possibly even indicating a form of genetic predeterminate for things of this nature, or even the much speculated 'psychic gene complex'. The latter might also explain the seemingly absurd claims of 'witch blood' and 'sacred lineages' found in certain popular books, particularly if the gene was recessive, as well as the even more superstitious claims of the ritual transmission of such . But such speculations are impossible to test at this time. Though I suspect a variety of influences are at work here.

Applying all this to scholarly accounts of the Knights Templar, as well as sensible critiques of the popular books in the genre, I developed the thesis of the book. As the seven hundredth anniversary of the Templar's suppression approached and the Vatican announced the release of its secret papers on the Order I decided this book had to be written.

The story as presented is not intended to affirm or censure what the

Knights Templars were, or what they believed. It is certainly not intended to romanticize them but merely to record. Like any human association they contained all aspects of humanity, both good and bad and all points in between. At best their beliefs, like those of any of us, were a mere grappling with a mystery in the dark, producing a faith, part true, part illusion. But perhaps what we can celebrate about them is that which I believe was their core ethos, no matter how narrowly they applied it, the love of liberty and the fight for the emancipation from servitude.

I hope this book will appeal both to the novice who will learn much about certain esoteric English traditions within it, and the adept who can read between its lines.

---

1 Following their contact with the St Leger family, a common preoccupation within the Westcote family seems to have been an interest in religious sects, often centred on various forms of baptism. Something eventually leading up to the Baptist movement itself. The same people were also often Freemasons in later centuries. One famous member of this line was Bishop B F Westcott, 19th century theologian, Hermeticist and founder of the Cambridge Ghost Club (proto SPR). Another family closely related to the Wescotes were the Stuckleys, who produced that 'Arch Druid', William Stukeley, surveyor of England's great megaliths. Those that crossed the Atlantic ocean spawned Catherine Westcott Tingley, effectively the founder of the American Theosophical movement. But the most famous member of this line was probably Wynn Westcott, one of the founders of the Hermetic Order of Golden Dawn.

The Black Knights

The Black Knights

The Birth of the Templars

According to orthodox historians, the Knights Templar were a devout Catholic order founded by French knight Hugues de Payens, with his kinsman Godfrey de Saint-Omer, both veterans of the First Crusade. In 1119 they had proposed the creation of a monastic military order for the protection of pilgrims in the Holy Land. King Baldwin II of Jerusalem agreed to their request and gave them a headquarters in Jerusalem, on the Temple Mount, from which they took their name, the Poor Fellow-Soldiers of Christ and of the Temple of Solomon. The Order was self styled as the exemplar of perfect Christian chivalry and with the backing of St Bernard of Clairvaux and the monastic Cistercian Order, operated under the authority of the Pope alone, giving them almost complete local autonomy. Inundated with pious donations of land and money

The Black Knights

the Order became wealthy and was soon inventing an early form of international banking. The Order grew in wealth and power, till it became one of the richest institutions in Europe, with property across the entire Continent. In 1306, after evoking the fear and envy of the ambitious French King Phillip le Bel, the Order was falsely accused and persecuted and was eventually dissolved by a coerced Pope in 1312, with its French leadership executed soon after. In reality however there is far more to the Templars than just this.

In contrast to this official story we have extraordinary modern claims about the alleged secret activities of the Templars, ranging from them being the secret custodians of the Holy Grail, in a wide variety of manifestations, to their status as an occult society, which somehow surviving their dissolution and even a Gnostic sex cult! These modern legends have shaped the public perception of the Knights Templar, particularly through recent books such as the Holy Blood and the Holy Grail and The Da Vinci Code, or via the various pseudo Neo-Templar Orders. They are of course mostly fantasy.

The purpose of this book is to unearth the truth behind the legends and to unveil a thesis which shows how both of these extreme positions contain both an element of truth and a delusional distortion. It will particularly show how the facts are, as should be expected, far more complex than either. It will also specifically focus on the history of the Templars in England, which reveals

The Black Knights

some surprising facts about the Order. In part it will also frame its conclusions in light of the new testimony revealed in the so-called Chinon document. Newly released confidential confessions made to the Pope's representatives in 1308, by those Templars who had been imprisoned and tortured at Chinon.

So where do the Templars really begin? Let's first look a little closer at some of its alleged founders. Hughes de Payen is believed to have been of Burgundian descent, though he was born at Château Payens, about ten kilometres from Troyes, in Champagne. He was therefore the vassal of Count Hugh of Champagne, with whom he probably took part in the First Crusade. The Count had returned to Jerusalem again in 1108, accompanied by Hugues and assorted friends, who remained there after the Count went back to France. It is said de Payen then organized nine monk-knights to defend pilgrims in the Holy Land, in response to the call for action by the Cluniac Pope Urban II. How nine monks were supposed to do this is a mystery to many and raises the possibility of it being a 'cover story' rather than a real mission. We only know of eight of these knights and all are usually said to have been relatives of de Payen, by blood or marriage, though this is difficult to prove. But certainly the majority were Burgundian or Flemish, as were many leading Templars up until the time of the Order's dissolution.

The concept of either monks taking up arms, or knights taking holy orders, was considered outrageous by many at the time. Monks were hypocritically encouraged to bless knights entering into

The Black Knights

battle but were themselves supposed to be pacifists. The notion that violence could be combined with spirituality had not been heard of since the time of the Viking warrior cults. Though remnants of these cults were believed to have still existed in some form, particularly amongst the Nordic and later Saxon, members of the elite Varangian Guard – Nordic mercenary troops organised into a fanatical bodyguard by the late Byzantine Roman Empire. It is thus possible that these were an influence. There is even the slight possibility that certain aspects of the ancient cult of Mithras may have been preserved in the Byzantine Roman army, in some Christianised form perhaps. If preserved within the old Roman Imperial Guard this could have been inherited by the Varangians as well and absorbed. This point will become significant later.

But a more immediate source was the Catholic call for a holy military order, the 'Knights of Christ', answerable only to the Pope, which would become the exemplar of Christian chivalry. St Bernard would become one of the most vociferous champions of this idea. The Knights Templar were the first order to appropriate this ideal, even the Knights Hospitallers of St John, a slightly earlier monastic crusading order, did not take up military arms until later, following the Templar's example. However It is quite likely they would have done eventually, even without the Templar's initiative. Perhaps an important consideration in the latter's plans if they differed from the orthodoxy of Rome and feared it's consequences.

More broadly there was a greater ideal emerging, the notion that the state of things could never be changed externally until inner personal transformation had occurred and that this inner change

The Black Knights

could not be complete until the external social conditions were in place to support it. Thus inner and outer work were rightly seen as closely entwined, a new notion that had been imported from the Orient. Alas though, for the medieval European mind outer transformation usually meant invasion and colonisation and inner work was typically associated with Christian devotion. Thus the idea of the knight-monk was born.

The name de Payens is often translated as 'pagan' and this is most likely the correct etymology, however it is important to realise that Hughes was named after his family and their residence not his personal inclinations. Thus all the family born on the de Payen estate were de Payens regardless of their beliefs. Claims that this indicates he was a pagan are thus a naïve over simplification. However the family name does seem to have been derived from the term 'pagan', which may in fact be significant. What it reveals may be elucidated by those apparently contemporary descriptions of Hughes de Payen, as raven haired and of dark complexion, something revealed in the well circulated portrait of him.[1] This dark complexion was not uncommon in the region and is normally explained by the intermarriage of Europeans with Moors. Surprisingly for many the a large number of Iberians were interracial in this way. The majority of the Muslim population of Andalusia was in fact European in origin, largely from Visigothic stock, who had converted to Islam out of economic and social convenience and had sometimes intermarried with Moorish families. Their kin who remained Christian were termed Mozarabs

The Black Knights

and were tolerated by the relatively liberal Islamic society of the Cordoba Caliphate. This culture itself consisting on an eclectic mix of Sunni Islam with various schools of Sufi mysticism and a tinge of Jewish Kabbalah (that had even absorbed certain Christian mystical themes). In this melting pot the Christian Mozarabs had also adopted Kabbalistic and Islamic notions, such as the veneration of the 'Divine Feminine'.[2] Later with the collapse of the Caliphate and its invasion by Islamic Fundamentalists, all non-Muslims and some Muslims, were persecuted and many crossed the Pyrenees seeking sanctuary and a new settlement. Significantly the term 'pagan' in this period simply meant 'non-Christian' and was more often applied to Jews and Muslims than anyone else. Even Christians tinged with such non Christian views might be labelled 'pagan'.[3] This suggests that the de Payen family probably originally arrived from Iberian Peninsula. If so a Moorish origin would indicate the Templar's associations with the Orient and its culture go back further than anyone previously suspected.

Hugh's main companion was Godfrey of Saint-Omer, a knight from Flanders. It was said that these two were so poor on arriving in Jerusalem they had to share a horse, thus giving rise to the image on Templar seals of two knights on one horse. This however is simply absurd, as all knights had to have, at the very least, a riding horse, the palfrey or 'courser' and a reserved battle horse, the dexterarius or 'high horse', simply to function at all. What this seal may really have indicated remains a mystery and the popular claim that it indicates two faces of the Order actually have some truth to it,

The Black Knights

but we shall return to this later. The fact that these knights were from Burgundy and Flanders also typifies the close connections between these two regions and the interrelatedness of their families.

The third most important knight was Andre de Montbard, the uncle of St Bernard of Clairvaux, who I suspect drew his older nephew into a 'Templar plot' in an ingenious way as we shall see. The others, Payen de Montdidier, Archambaud de St. Agnan, Geoffrey Bison and two men referred to only as Rossal and Gondamer, are largely forgotten to history and are now little more than mysterious names. The ninth knight remains completely unknown, some suggest he was a collective figure representing the group soul of the eight knights, a kind of entity magicians call an egregore. But circumstantial evidence indicates he may in fact have been the Count of Champagne himself, Hugh's feudal lord 4 If so he was clearly the mastermind behind the Templars and de Payen merely his agent, albeit one given a great degree of creative freedom. In this secret relationship of a public Grand Master of the Order and a secret aristocratic mastermind, the ninth knight, we may get a first glimpse of the real structure of the Knights Templar and understand the real meaning of their seal. The Templars were not controlled by a secret inner circle, but rather by a secret outer one.

It is said that the Templars remained as nine knights for nine years, until their incorporation into the Church as a Catholic Order at the Council of Troyes in 1128. If they really were protecting pilgrims all this time it seems an unlikely claim. However before we reject

The Black Knights

this completely we should bear in mind that a Templar military unit did not just consist of its knights, for every one of these there were three Templar sergeants, making up the number to at least 36 (or maybe 33 if we discount the absent Count) and for each of these Templars there were at least three local mercenary troops under their control, typically Turkish horse archers by the mid 12th century. So we have a potential garrison of well over a hundred troops. In addition to these were the squires of the knights who could also take on a combative role. It was for this reason that in the medieval period the smallest band of knights – a unit under a baron signified by the arms or banner he carried – was arbitrarily said to be ten, or in terms of the preceeding, forty loyal men. Even so, this is still a small number for the stated mission of total pilgrim guard, but perhaps the Templars were acting more as a selective bodyguard in this period, probably escorting elite pilgrims between, or at, specific sites. This in itself would have been fairly light work and left the knights plenty of free time. Later of course their military role would expand into a kind of medieval special forces regiment (with no doubt the usual attendant hype boosting their alleged prowess), clearing the way for the larger battalions, as well as assisting the king in the strategic planning of military operations in the region. At the height of their fame and power their numbers would increase dramatically and at their height they were able to field some 600 knights, giving them an estimated strength of over 5000 men. Close examination of their Rule indicates they were first and foremost a military order groomed for combat not contemplation.

The Black Knights

But we are jumping ahead of ourselves. Why exactly did these people go to Jerusalem in the first place? Simply to become private security guards? Or was there a deeper agenda? One clue is found in the letter sent to Andre Montbard's uncle, St Bernard of Clairvaux, by Hughes de Payen. Many people have made the mistake of thinking that St Bernard was an influence on the Templar's ideology, but this is not the case. St Bernard simply supported the popular desire within the Papal establishment to see the creation of what became known as the 'Knights of Christ', that religious order of solders in the service of God alone, or at least his vicar the Pope. Such an Order would have to be the highest example of Christian chivalry, standing in sharp contrast with the contemporary class of knighthood, which Saint Bernard had denounced as lawless bandits and heathens, claiming the Crusades had served Europe by emptying it of them. It has even been plausibly suggested that one hidden agenda of the Crusades was not the liberation of the Holy Land, but the deliberate liberation of Europe from such elements! De Payen's letter to Bernard portrayed the Templars as just this kind of exemplary knighthood and he was clearly trying to fill this role in the eyes of the Abbot, as well as the Pope, who was also naturally quite keen on gaining a private army. The ploy seems to have worked and Saint Bernard eagerly accepted the claims of the new Order, writing a public letter praising them, which was circulated across Europe permanently associating the Templars with the idea of the Knights of Christ. It was thus not long before the Pope accepted them as such, though it

The Black Knights

was not until 1128 that they were officially installed as a Catholic institution and given their Cistercian Rule, written by St Bernard himself. Sometime after this three Papal bulls were also issued, awarding the Templars a white mantle and later a red cross, on their request, as well as the authority to hold their own services and rites. More significantly they were effectively given virtual autonomy, in that the only power over them was to be the Pope, represented by the Grand Master of the Order in day to day affairs. But as the Pope was generally rather busy and distant from local events, it was the Grand Master who held the actual absolute power, free from the more regional authority of kings and archbishops.

To some extent this tied them to the Vatican, but only in ways of no importance to them (such as their duty to house and assist papal envoys) and they had many excuses when Papal support did not suit their objectives. The very same strategy had been earlier successfully applied by the monastic Cluniac Order, who were to become the Templar's main rivals. The Templars were seldom original, they merely adopted the most intelligent strategies of others, cleverly combining them.

Later the Templars also gained so much control over the Vatican's finances and influence in its diplomatic missions, that they essentially controlled the Popes themselves, placing their own supporters close to him and so even freed themselves from this authority. But perhaps of greatest importance to the Order was the fact that their autonomy also made them exempt from taxation and levies of all kinds and immune to local religious authority,

The Black Knights

particularly from the Church's power of excommunication.

Many historians have simply taken this at face value, suggesting that the knights really were a devout order and that the whole Templar mission to Jerusalem was designed to put themselves in a position from which they could be chosen as the desired Knights of Christ, as the de facto guardians of the holiest shrines, bolstered by the fact that the Pope had first requested this task undertaken. Essentially correct, but the only thing that's wrong with this thesis is that the Templars were anything but such exemplary Christian knights, as there is no evidence that they were anything other than typical Crusaders, that is that they were essentially low ranking nobles out for plunder and booty. There is even gossip that they were worse than most, with the sarcastic phrase 'as drunk as a Templar' common in Germany. While many others regarded them as the frequent clients of prostitutes. In Germany, which seems to have had a particularly low opinion of them, the term Tempelhaus also meant brothel and a place were abortions could be procured. Thus it was no coincidence that behind Templar run St Sepulchre's church in London - the place Crusaders visited for blessings immediately before heading off to the Holy Land - lay the aptly named Cock Lane, one of the earliest legal 'red light' districts of Medieval Europe, fulfilling an important secular function there.

Many contemporary commentators refused to accept this image of the Templars, no doubt awed by the public relations coup pulled off by uncle Bernard. However the new Chinon documents clearly reveal the secret sex lives of the knights, which like most all male

The Black Knights

institutions would have included homosexual practise. Here we read of Templar Raymond de Caron explaining he was instructed to 'preserve purity and chastity', but if he could not do so 'things were better done secretly than publicly'. As well as Hugo de Perraud declare that it was 'imposed on them to abstain from all contact with women, but that, if they were unable to restrain their lust, they should join themselves with brothers of their Order'. This should not be a shock to most people, nor is it intended to scandalize, it is simply an acceptance of reality. Though one later selectively used against the knights by their enemies. Moreover, it has also been plausibly suggested that the knights were a kind of medieval foreign legion, something those who needed to escape Europe in a hurry could join and avoid difficult situations. The Order was also said to be an easy haven for heretics, given the total immunity from local excommunication they received within it. The Templars even seemed to go out of their way to attract heretics and outlaws, as some court records demonstrate - particularly in Somerset it seems - no doubt trading protection for obedience, when available manpower was lacking and duplicity rampant.

A further attraction that was to become an advantage in joining the Templars was that they were among the first chivalric orders to allow a social mobility. Trusted squires could be made sergeants and particularly worthy sergeants might be dubbed knights and even take monastic vows. Thus launching the whole sordid business of moral hypocrisy amongst the socially ambitious that is all too common today.

The Black Knights

The Templar's strict Cistercian Rule is often quoted as evidence of their piety, the interesting thing about this rule however is its last clause, which clearly states that the Grand Master can override any of the prior rules on the grounds of local custom and convention. Thus it should come as no surprise that many Templars should be depicted as long haired, sometimes clean shaven and wearing pointed Arabic footwear. In direct contravention of their rules, that insist a Templar be short haired, bearded and refrain from oriental dress and customs. We have already seen how flexible the knights were with their rules regarding sex. The only rules that seemed to be taken seriously were those that instilled discipline deemed necessary for an effective fighting unit, which is all most of the Templars were. The general ethos of the rules themselves seems to be one of a machismo and the repression of femininity and sexuality, required of killing machines (a curious pragmatic contradiction given the ethos of the cult they protected). This is not to say the Templars never took any of their more religious vows seriously, or did not value the feminine, no doubt some did, particular amongst the higher ranks, confraternities and patrons, just that this aspect was not an important requirement for the front-line troops. Though it was not a redundant aspect either of course, as even those with a less than illustrious past were no doubt regardable as souls in need of salvation and discipline and probably fell into this role eagerly as do many reforming criminals and rehab clients even today.

So if they were not really the 'Knights of Christ' as advertised, what

The Black Knights

the hell was going on? Was it all just simply a matter of naïve idealisation and hypocrisy or was there something more complex going on? I think the answer was twofold, one, the agenda was to create an autonomous institution relatively free of the power of the King and any regional Church authority; and two, to create an efficient, absolutely loyal military force, that would unswervingly serve those who governed the Order and those who benefited from its social and financial privileges. The period of the early Templars was one of social change, particularly in France, where the monarchy was then enthusiastically developing the new concept of a centralised Kingdom, in emulation of Charlemagne's old Neo-Romanism. In conscious opposition to the traditional, decentralised, Feudal society of the barons. Likewise the powerful Cluniac Order, centred on Burgundy, had become a Church within the Church and was pushing for a universal Christian Theocracy. It being no coincidence that a Cluniac Pope Urban II had launched the Crusades. This early form of Christian Fundamentalism, albeit of a curious millennially, mystical kind, also sought to eradicate all heresy and create a universal doctrine and pious culture. It is very significant in this respect that many early Templars appear to be Burgundians in exile. Perhaps having first hand experience of the Cluniacs. Independent nobles like the Count of Champagne, the richest man in France at the time, would have also been keen to preserve their independence from both the French King and the Church and so be obvious backers of any organised attempt at such autonomy. The composition of the early Templars makes a great deal of sense in this respect. It is not hard to imagine how

The Black Knights

those seeing the potential immanent emergence of a dangerous military order backing a Cluniac agenda, or supporting Christian kings, would seek to coopt it for their own benefit. Or that later orders would arise with either a Templar or Cluniac orientation, or some hybrid of both. The Templar agenda is very clear when we look at their effect on history though. Thus the public piety of the Templars, in effect a holy fraud to make their objectives politically possible, has to be seen in this context. Much in the same way as today's politicians often fake religious faith in order to succeed in a conservative environment. That said, it will soon become clear that Templars, or rather their masters, did have their own religious doctrine, albeit one many in Rome may not have approved.

At the root of the Templar Order, as with any similar institution, was of course the desire for power. Given the background of those behind them, this desired power seems to have originally been for the independence of the aristocracy from all outside influence, taxation and regulation. For as we have seen it was at this time that not only was the Church deepening its socio-political hold across much of Europe, but also a time when many monarchs were emulating the French in creating the first centralised Nation States and innevitable attendant bureaucracies, often at the cost of heavy taxation. All of this was an anathema to most independently minded nobles with their own little fiefdoms. The only exception of course being those who were offered powerful roles in the new bureaucracy, a growing trend as the power of State and Church expanded. Later the Templars themselves became embroiled in this very evolution, perhaps shrewdly recognising it as then

The Black Knights

unstoppable. But even here their support always seems to have been for the most 'hands off' of potential monarchs and in favour of new democratic institutions, albeit for the privileged classes..

How this was actually achieved can be seen when we examine the secular aspects of the Templars. The classic image of the Knight Templar, as a white clad warrior leading an elite host of knights in war and peace is something of a misleading half truth. In war the bulk of a Templar force would have been mercenaries recruited locally, just as many of their low level administrators and scribes were often Saracens. Those who converted to Christianity were able to rise through the Templar ranks being seen as no different to eastern educated Europeans (with even the part Syrian Phillip of Nablus becoming the seventh Grand Master of the Order in 1170.[5]). In addition to these Templar associates were armed esquires who provided an infantry and security force and Templar sergeants who constituted a light cavalry. These were the Templars who were functioning on a day to day basis as guardians of the Holy Land and were recruited as much locally as they were in Europe.

The Templar Knights were merely an 'officer class' who planned and oversaw operations, taking part in battle themselves only in major engagements, in which they constituted the front-line heavy cavalry, and often took the glory. Similarly in peace time a Templar estate consisted mostly of indigenous farmers and craftsman, along with serving esquires who acted as intermediaries for the knights. Low level administrators and sergeants ran things at a planning level. With the Templars themselves acted like typical feudal aristocracy who mostly let their staff get on with their work, as long

The Black Knights

as they remained loyal. As the Order grew these knight-monks took on the work of diplomats and the financial business of the Order and let their estates effectively manage themselves. It has been shown through a study of the Orders demographics that most of the 'knights' outside of the Holy Land were quite old and of low rank in the nobility, at least by the latter years of the Order. The exception in England being on the Welsh and Scottish borders, where the Templars were engaged in the military activities on behalf of the English king against the 'rebellious Celtic fringes'.

But most importantly in addition to this core institution and its appendages were what were called secular or lay knights, who joined one of the several different kinds of Templar Confraternities. These were simply knights who had not taken religious vows and would not become monks, but desired to serve the Order solely in a military or administrative capacity. For a small fee these knights became associate members of the Templars and qualified for most of their privileges. They were not allowed to wear the white mantel, being 'profane' and so were awarded a black mantle of 'sin' instead, emblazoned with the Templar red cross to signify their allegiance. While these knights were originally considered lower ranking than the Templar knights proper and technically could not hold positions of authority within the Order, they were none the less of the knightly class and held all the social authority that entailed, as well as gaining other important roles. Moreover, as time went on and manpower dwindled lay knights were eventually allowed positions of authority within the Order.

The Black Knights

Now, what is interesting about these 'Black Knights' as we might call them is that where as most monastic Templars tended to come from the lower nobility, or be the younger sons of the higher aristocracy, these secular knights came from a variety of backgrounds, and were sometimes wealthy, influential nobles. The extreme case in point being the Count of Champagne himself. Their social status gave them something of an unofficial authority. Even at the height of the Order, after the Templars became more organised under Blanchard, they were eligible to become 'advisors' to their regional Masters, as well as the Grand Master himself, within Councils established to help them govern effectively. This Council was also largely responsible for selecting of the electoral college (eight knights, four sergeants, one chaplain) who elected the heirs to the Grand Master and would install them in power, with the tacit approval of often disinterested monarchs and popes. It is my contention that these wealthy 'black knights' were the real power behind the Order. Not an inner circle but an outer one, 'riding behind' the official Grand Master. A reality perhaps also behind the oddity of the Templar banner, the famous beauseant, consisting of a black band over the white band, a somewhat odd symbolism for a Christian Order. Curiously a self professed psychic I once met at the Templar church, told me he had seen black clad knights sitting on the left hand, north side of the church. While white clad Templars sat to their south, on the right of the aisle, reproducing the banner. This was perhaps pure fantasy, but oddly the same seating arrangement is today used by members of the Middle and Inner Temple respectively.

The Black Knights

In addition to their influence within the Order, many of these secular Templars were also wealthy landowners and as such had donated a significant amount of property and wealth to the Temple. It was through such donations that the Order had grown rich and even later on when their riches were also based on the creative use of this wealth, such as early banking and money lending, the favour of the landed aristocracy was still crucial for them. This noble allegiance is also evidenced through the local battles of the Order. Within France the Templars, and their associates, were associated with defending the independence of local communities and their lords, from monarchical interference. While in Britain, although they seem to have taken both sides during the Baron's Revolt, their influence was generally found in favour of the Feudal lords. Though they are also quite notable for their backing of those monarchs who supported a more traditional feudalism, or those who espoused even greater liberality. In this respect they were also very instrumental in the creation and preservation of the Magna Carta [6], with up to as well as the first Baronial parliaments. Thus we see how the aforementioned socio-political agenda worked. For these rich secular knights and their even wealthier supporters, acquired many of the privileges and immunities of the Templars and could easily benefit from those rights technically granted only to the knight-monks, who effectively acted as their private army. The extent to which those at the top were known remains uncertain, some candidates such as the Marshall family seem to have made their support for the Templars well known. Others however appear to have remained in the shadows and

The Black Knights

worked through certain intermediaries in the Confraternities, such as the St Legers.

Finally, the cultural innovations of the Templars, mostly imported from the Orient, could also be seen as based on their desire to retain power, as well as a quest for further independence and well being for themselves and their communities. Innovations such as the gradual accumulation and manipulation of capital, both individual and collective; the acquisition of original knowledge; and developments in technology, craft and the arts, all fit this context. All of which could be regarded as ennobling and liberating from external constraints, for those with the right access. This in itself was one of the most important legacies of the Templars, which later would find a broader application.

However beyond all this there was clearly something more than mere secular ambition involved and it is to this that we now turn.

1. The portrait (http://en.wikipedia.org/wiki/Image:De_paynes.jpg) is alas of uncertain origin, the author's research has yet to find the source of this image and answers to enquiries have not been forthcoming. There are claims made that it is based on a contemporary description, however such descriptions have not been sourced. It remains a possibility that the picture is of modern origin, if this was the case it is still an interesting item as it hints that the artist has reached this same Moorish conclusion based on unstated evidence.

2. A point of detail is important here and one that may shed some very interesting light on the history of the Templars. One of the most influential elements of this Moorish culture to enter Christian Europe was the reverence for the 'female aspect' of divinity. This is believed to have been introduced by the Mozarabs, whose unique form of the Mass consisted of its emphasis on the Virgin Mary and the breaking of the communion bread into nine pieces, reflecting nine aspects of Christ. Nine itself being a lunar number. It was also spread via mystical Sufi love

The Black Knights

poetry, which emphasised a devotion to this feminine principle and its recapture after loss, that would greatly influence the Troubadours (though social conditions in Feudal Europe often made their tale's conclusions more pessimistic). The popularity of the Black Madonnas further echo this influence. Even St Bernard himself would take up the image, or perhaps recuperate it for the Church. In his adoption of a very Platonic and oddly misogynistic, form of it in his cult of the Virgin Mary. A common objection to this thesis is that Moorish Spain was essentially Sunni, a sect of Islam that did not revere the feminine. However due to the influence of Sufism in the Cordoba Caliphate it was probably introduced heretically. A deeper source of this image however, which had also informed Sunni Sufis, such as Ibn Arabi and Ibn Sena, where the mystical archetypes of the Ismailian Shia sects and the imagery of poetry that they spread from Shia Persia. Here the image of Fatima, the daughter of Mohamed and mother of his descendants, had been used as a vessel for more ancient goddess images and given a mystical spin. These ideas were introduced into Andalusia by Ismaili missionaries, themselves often agents of secret societies working for the rival Fatimid Empire of North Africa, who were no doubt contacting disaffected elements in Moorish Spain. Even deeper the Iberian coast lands were long ago once Phoenician, or Carthaginian, whose ancient goddess Tanit, a form of Astarte, was said to have borne local versions of the Greek gods Apollo and Dionysos, by Baal or El, just as Fatima had borne Hasan and Hasayn by Ali. Thus it comes as no surprise to find the talisman known as the Hand of Fatima in some Arab regions, known as the Hand of Tanit in Spain. Indicating the web of myth that underlay the powerful image of the Divine Feminine. One which found further correspondence in Europe, not only in semi pagan goddess survivals, like St Bride, but also in the parallels drawn by Sufis between Fatima as an archetype and the Virgin Mary and more particularly Mary Bethany, who at the time was conflated with Mary Magdalene. The fingers of the Hand were associated with Muhammed, Ali, Fatima, Hasan and Hasayn in Islamic folklore and with metaphysical principles by the Ismailis. As well as perhaps with the Baals, Tanit and the Carthaginian Dionysos and Apollo in an earlier pagan version. Local pagan and Christian variants, if any were developed, would not be hard to imagine.

3. It has often been claimed that pagan simply meant 'country dweller' and indeed the French term for peasant, paysan, is derived from this. However this was a Roman term, by the medieval period the term had shifted its meaning. The de Payen family were also anything but peasants.

4. A letter to Hugh from the Bishop of Chartres, dated at 1114, congratulates him on his joining the Militia of Christ, as the Templars were widely known. It is not until 1124 however that he officially joined the Order as a lay associate, or 'Black Knight'. But it would be totally inconceivable that he would pledge obedience to his own vassal.

The Black Knights

5. Phillip of Nablus was certainly half Syrian culturally, having been born in Syria and educated by hired Saracens. There were also rumours that his real father was secretly of Arabian origin.

6. At least 13 of the 24 signatories of the Magna Carta, and rebel leaders, were closely associated with the Templars and one of the Marshall sons was a dominant influence among them, along with Earl Robert de Vere. While Earl Marshall himself was perhaps the closest of King John's advisors, when the monarch was 'safely' housed in the New Temple in London. Details of the signatories and their familial alliances will be found in a forthcoming companion book to this introductory work. But include two de Clares, a Marshall, two Bigods, a Percy, a de Vere, a de Lacy, a Mowbray and of course Robert de Ros and Geoffrey de Mandeville.

The Black Knights

The Hidden Roots of the Templars

The Templars as a monastic order were first and foremost founded on theological grounds. Their crusade to the Holy Land, then seen as the spiritual heart of Christendom and the 'centre of creation', is the most obvious indication of this. Of course the Crusades were a complex mix of both religious and secular ambition, as well as at a lower level the main attraction for a barbarous horde, seeking divine favour or booty. However the Templars as an order were a little more intelligent than most and seem somewhat different in their behaviour than the others of their ilk. An authentic faith is clearly present with many of them as we shall see, at least amongst the upper ranks of the Order. Most notably they displayed several religious tendencies that differed from their peers. Such fringe beliefs unsanctioned by Rome were hardly the fodder of the conformist Roman Catholic and least of all something the wise Machiavellian would risk associating with. One of the most striking

The Black Knights

of these idiosyncrasies is the presence of the mythical figure of Abraxas on several Templar seals. This Abraxas was an ancient Gnostic Aeon - some say Archon - revered by Basildeans, a second century sect of Hellenic Egypt. Represented as a solar deity, with a rooster's head and serpentine legs, or mouthed tentacles, the Aeon Abraxas symbolised the intelligence of the totality of the created Cosmos (the Solar System and Imperium then), with its seven archetypal planetary components and a name that added numerologically to 365.[1] By the early Middle Ages however Abraxas was generally regarded as a demonic being in the service of Satan. Though it might also have been regarded as an astrological talisman by Hermeticists. But whether we interpret this image as a heretical Gnostic relic, an evil Satanic demon, or a magical talisman, the key point is it is certainly nothing a devout Christian would associate with. It is an extremely bizarre symbol to use. Some have suggested that the image represented a harmless personal symbol, or a heraldic device, much as other sinister beings were used, such as dragons or mermaids. However even if we accept this unlikely scenario it cannot be claimed of another fringe preoccupation of the Order, the Black Madonnas.

The Cult of the Black Madonna was one of the most popular in medieval Europe, yet despite this it was viewed with suspicion by Rome as a resurgence of heathen belief. This was because the cult, centred on the reverence of ebony statues, nominally of the Virgin

The Black Knights

A Templar Abraxas Seal

The Black Knights

Mary, often emerged in former centres of pagan goddess worship. This reverence, that bordered on idolatry for many in the Church, usually took place in crypts or subterranean caverns dedicated to the Madonna and even when above ground was associated with sacred wells, standing stones and deep rooted ancient trees, all regarded as gates to the underworld by pagans. In his book *The Cult of the Black Virgin*, Ean Begg, plausibly traces these images back to the cult of Cybele and the dark aspects of Artemis, Isis and Athena. In pagan mythos such 'dark aspects' represented not only the chthonic, but also the deep, dark ocean and the dark night sky, both metaphoric of great voids, which were regarded as primal 'wombs' from which all things manifested. The black goddess was thus a creatrix, the term 'dark' in this context having no moral significance. Though a notion of primality was often associated with this point of origin. Later in more philosophic and Gnostic times the dark image came to be associated with the wisdom aspects of various goddesses and with gnostic Sophia, the archetype of divine wisdom, in particular. Its later medieval manifestation was a popular, grassroots one in the main, but had also influenced such an important and seemingly sympathetic Church figure as Saint Bernard, who quoted the famous line from the biblical Song of Solomon, in many of his sermons, 'I am black but comely, o ye daughters of Jerusalem'. Seemingly indicating how these originally pagan images had been absorbed into popular Christianity. St Bernard was an exception however and so were his associates the Templars, who were also linked with these shrines, through their policing the pilgrimage routes to and from them, just as in the East.

The Black Knights

If the Templars were harbouring unorthodox religious viewpoints like this what did they really believe in? Further clues emerge when we look at the nature of the Court of Troyes from which they first emerged. According to the authors of the Holy Blood and the Holy Grail, this court held an 'influential school of Cabbalistic and esoteric study'. This is partly true, but it is a claim to be treated with caution, as we read in the chapter notes on this statement, the school was actually that of Rabbi Rashi founded in 1070.[2] Now the Rashi school did contain an esoteric element and one that most likely included Iberian Kabbalists, but this was a fringe element and Rashi himself was far more interested in orthodox Talmudic study. However even the presence of such a school was testament to the tolerance of the court in a time when rabid anti-Semitism was the norm in much of Europe. Another exception of course being Moorish Spain where Jews were welcome and Sufi mysticism had revitalised the schools of Kabbalism. Just as they would Christian mysticism, until the collapse of the Caliphate.

What is undeniably true is that Troyes was charged with a mystical air, one that also manifest in the patronage Hugh of Champagne gave to Saint Bernard's reform of the Cistercian Order. The Cistercians themselves were a particularly ascetic brotherhood, who some have claimed originally bordered on Gnosticism. Certainly under Bernard's reform they became even more mystical and seem to have some relation to the Cluniac Order of Burgundy. Bernard taught the Transcendental ascent of the Soul through Love in his sermons on the Song of Solomon, emphasizing a new

The Black Knights

mysticism devoted to the Virgin Mary as a symbol of Divine Love. He was as such the first major promoter of the Cult of Mary, seen by many as a return of feminine spirituality to Christianity. It was largely due to this zealous promotion that the Virgin Mary became central to Catholicism. Though Marianism has an older pedigree on the fringes of ancient Christianity. Unfortunately Bernard's take on the Marian Mysteries was entirely Idealised and Platonic however and in everyday life he was not adverse to a certain degree of misogyny.

Perhaps the apex of the influence of this court on early Medieval spirituality was as the home of Chrétien de Troyes. Who between 1160 and 1172, was the earliest known writer of the classic Arthuriad and whose cycle of tales climaxed with the first written account of the Holy Grail, 'Perceval, le Conte du Graal', sometime after 1180. The Grail story was actually written when Chrétien was under the patronage of Count Phillip of Flanders, from whom he claimed inspiration. Given the connection between Flanders and Britain after 1066, particularly its Celtic fringes, it likely that this was partly true. However it is also likely that the story contained a deeper mystery taught to Chrétien at Troyes. To understand the essence of this we have to look at his earlier works and in particular his patron Marie of Champagne.

Marie was the daughter of Eleanor of Aquitaine and it is the mother who is a key figure in this history. Eleanor became one of the most powerful and charismatic personalities of feudal Europe. Married to King Louis of France at a young age in 1137, Eleanor was already

The Black Knights

an enthusiastic supporter of the cult of Courtly Love popularised by the Troubadours. A cult that had emerged in her native court of Aquitaine in the late 11th century. This tradition was initially one of both an erotic sexual liberation, from the rigid conventions of medieval Christianity and also at the same time a subtle psychic sublimation of sexuality with transcendental aims. A complex tangle of moral and psychological contradictions, it also sought to overcome the limits of dualism. Later the cult became more romanticised and less erotic, creating the model for romantic love from then on. It is widely believed that the cult was inspired by the love poetry and Sufi mysticism of Moorish Spain, expressed in a more restrained Christian context. A central feature of the cult was an alluring female figure who becomes an unobtainable object of adoration. This on one hand led to a raised status and liberation for medieval women, but on the other to their objectification and distance, the first patriarchal idealisation of the feminine. It was almost certainly this culture that also revived Marianism, in the form of a far more Platonic variant of the cult and inspired Bernard of Clairvaux to champion the Virgin Mary and her Divine Love. While the radical liberational aspects of the cult were central for Eleanor, she also came under the sway of Bernard's conservative preaching. In 1145 she led a contingent on the Second Crusade from Vézelay, the legendary burial site of Mary Magdalene, that included her troop of female bodyguards in full armour. It was said that Queen Eleanor appeared at Vézelay dressed like an Amazon galloping through the crowds on a white horse, urging them to join the crusade. Little transpired in this campaign, but Eleanor

The Black Knights

returned a mature woman. She soon annulled her marriage to the French King and married Henry II of England. Bringing her troubadours with her and spreading the cult to new audience, just as she did when she departed her first Court of Love to marry Louis. In 1170 she would establish her new Court in Poitiers, where William, the best known troubadour, had lived thirty years earlier; making it a hotbed of Courtly Love. Meanwhile Marie, her daughter by Louis, was in the Court of Champagne, where she had married the then count, doing much the same thing and inspiring Chrétien de Troyes in what was to become the Grail Cycle.

This was the culture that was just emerging in the region when the Templars set out to the Holy Land and would no doubt have a further influence on them when they returned. The influence was a two way thing as well, for a later Grail romance written by Wolfram von Eschenbach at the beginning of the 13th century cast the Order as 'Guardians of the Grail', after the author met them in Jerusalem. It thus seems highly likely that the Templars represented a similar manifestation of this emerging culture, particularly when we consider what happened in Jerusalem in their earliest period there.

There are various conflicting stories of events in Palestine. An interesting account of the first Templars arrival in Jerusalem was given by Walter Map, a kind of medieval tabloid journalist. This story is widely regarded as fanciful by historians, who prefer the more 'reliable' account of the Templar's foundation given by the more scholarly Guillaume of Tyre seventy years after the event.

The Black Knights

This is understandable though as Map differs sharply from the other local commentators. He was not the most reliable of narrators, being prone to sensational gossip, such as accounts of dragon sightings near the Temple Mount and Norman vampires rising from the grave in Hereford (tales of vampires being popular folklore in medieval Normandy). However he had close contact with the Court of Champagne so was never totally dismissible and his account does make a great deal of sense in the light of the other elements of our history. Furthermore recently discovered evidence is indicating his story may be more accurate than previously thought. He may therefore have revealed an important secret.

Map claimed in a short narrative that one Paganus (Hughes de Payen?) had arrived at the church of the Holy Sepulchre in Jerusalem with a small company of knights. At that time the church was under the custodianship of a group of monks known as the Order of the Holy Sepulchre. These monks were a mysterious brotherhood not affiliated with either the Church of Rome or Byzantium, who were essentially squatting the church with official toleration. They claimed to be descended from the original Jerusalem Church, founded by the surviving disciples of Christ, which is unlikely and are generally regarded as a product of the First Crusade. Though it is just possible they were the descendants of custodians known to have been established by Roman Emperor Constantine, who had built the church many centuries earlier. The monks took these knights on as a militia to guard the church, where they became known as the Knights of the Holy Sepulchre.[2] They are

The Black Knights

not specifically described as monk-knights at this point, just knights. But seem to have developed a reverence for this ancient church, if their later emulative building projects and seals are any indication. Though this may have been the case prior to their arrival of course, it not being their first time in Jerusalem.

When Jerusalem was resecured in the First Crusade, Godfroi, the first Crusader king, took it on himself to protect this church and this role had been passed on to King Baldwin his successor. According to Map, Baldwin first supported the knights in their protective role at the church. But all the sources agree that the knights were then housed in the 'Temple of Solomon' on Mount Moriah - as Temple Mount was then known - either by Baldwin or the monks who owned other properties in the vicinity. The 'Temple' was actually the stables of the old palace now used by the Crusader court, itself part of the Al Aqsa Mosque. The original Temple of Jerusalem was of course long gone, but still held a powerful place in the Crusaders imagination and accordingly the knights were renamed the Knights of the Temple of Solomon. The Knights of the Stables would have been a far less impressive title! But despite being named after such a historically significant place the Templars themselves showed very little initial interest in it. Contrary to Masonic myth they did not revere the Temple as such, or have any myths based upon it, all of which are 17th century fantasies at best. Neither are the more modern stories true, that they were excavating on the Mount for some ancient holy artefact, be it the Ark of the Covenant or the Holy Grail.

While there is evidence of medieval excavation, the workings

The Black Knights

about 80 ft beneath the surface are simply not at the right level to have been targeted at any of these historical treasures, as several leading archaeologists have conformed. On the other hand these ancient shafts are somewhat mysterious. Excavated and explored during a survey by the British Royal Engineers in the 1860s, the workings were found to consist of a single main shaft from which radiated several horizontal tunnels that seemed to go nowhere. The discovery of Templar artefacts in the tunnels, including a small cross, as well as their connection with the partly subterranean stables used by the knights, led the expedition leader Warren (often described as an 'enthusiastic Freemason') to identify them as the work of the Order, constructed in their first nine years. Their purpose remained unknown, and popular speculation ranged from underground vaults for Templar gold, through secret ritual chambers, to incomplete access tunnels between sites. But Warren had missed some important evidence in all this (just as he did 20 years later as Metropolitan Police Commissioner during the Ripper Murders). The tunnels were in fact ancient water conduits taking water from the springs outside the city to the Mount. A few of the conduits had radiated directly beneath the mosque of the Dome of the Rock, on the top of Temple Mount, then converted into a church served by monks. Tradition had it that this was the site of the Holy of Holies of the Temple of Solomon and the path of the water conduits would seem to indicate this was so. Water was said to be supplied to this inner sanctum in all ancient descriptions of it. The Templars did show some interest in this site, representing it on their seals and it is alleged that it was also originally in the hands

The Black Knights

of the Order of the Holy Sepulchre and so may have come under their protection. But as we shall see it was not the building that they were interested in.

What is certain is soon after the Knights Templars arrived the monks of the Holy Sepulchre were absorbed into the Church and regularised as Augustinian Canons, making them official guardians for the Church of Rome. This regularisation was of course nominal and things become more interesting when we examine the history of these sites. The original church of the Holy Sepulchre was built by Constantine after the alleged 'discovery' there of the 'True Cross' and 'Tomb of Christ', by his mother the Empress and British Christian Helen [3]. Constantine was the first to tolerate Christianity and incorporate it as one of the many 'Solar cults' in his Imperial State religion of Sol Invictus, along with the cult of Helios Apollo, the Mysteries of Mithras, the Osirian sect and the original core rites of Baal and Astarte. Contrary to Roman Catholic propaganda Constantine was never a convert to Christianity, nor did he make Christianity the Roman State religion, being dedicated to Sol Invictus through out his life, as coins minted by him long after his alleged conversion prove. The claims of his biographer Bishop Eusebius probably being a later distortion of his vision of the god Apollo.[4] While Constantine did gradually shift to some form of Christianity, this occurred at the same time as he was becoming increasingly sexually repressive in both his laws and lifestyle. He also appears to have seen the organisational structure of the Church as an efficient bureaucracy and increasingly used it as so.

The Black Knights

Constantine's mother Helen claimed to have found the 'True Cross' on the hill on which her son built the Holy Sepulchre, marking it not only as the site of the Crucifixion for her, but also the burial place of Christ and therefore the site of the Resurrection. The church was thus seen as the centre of the Christian world and its inner sanctum was therefore built circular. The Templars, along with others, would later base many of their churches on this plan, creating the famous Templar round church.

Next to the site was a strange white rocky outcrop, apparently a former quarry, with two small sunken pits on one side giving it the appearance of a skull. This was identified as part of the hill of Golgotha on Christ was crucified. A tomb was also said to have been found. This vague identification is highly contentious however.

One piece of evidence against it is that the Gospels all insist the Crucifixion happened outside of the city walls, while the church is very clearly inside them (though this too is of course contended),[5] another flaw is that no independent evidence, or body of Jesus, or even a marked empty tomb has ever been found here! But the most interesting piece of counter evidence concerns the fact that the church was actually built on top of a Roman temple of Venus, built by Hadrian after the destruction of Jerusalem in 70 AD. Christians claim this pagan construction to have been the desecration of a Christian site, however the Romans rarely did this, more often than not they simply colonised an indigenous cult by overlaying it and its shrines with their own equivalent deity. In this case the implication would be that a temple of the 'Bride of God', Asherah,

The Black Knights

existed here before the fall of Jerusalem. While that may seem unlikely in the context of the strict Judaism of the time, it should be remembered that much earlier Solomon himself had included Asherah in the Temple and the Hellenized Jewish establishment had greatly desired the 're-paganisation' of Judea. If we allow the existence of a small temple to Asherah here we should also remember that Asherah was often equated with Astarte in this period, thus we return again to the cult of Sol Invictus. If the custodians of the church were descendants of those installed there by Constantine they may well have preserved a Christianised version of this mythos, no doubt held to be the 'true' foundation of Christianity. So did the Templars travel to the Holy Sepulchre to seek this tradition out? It is not hard to imagine a radical 'Marian' tradition seeking its 'pagan' origins while retaining its basic Christianity. These events happened immediately after the First Crusade, so contact had already been made with various groups in the region. Their connections with Constantine may go back even further as we shall see.

Another interesting feature of this mythos is the aspect of the Son-Lover of the Goddess. In the original Sol Invictus mythos this was El-Gabal, a Syrian Baal closely related to the biblical El (Elohim). Regarded in the Hellenised Syrian form of the cult as both the Consort and the Son of the Goddess, in early historical times he took a central role as a paternal deity, with the Goddess as his consort. In the Roman development his solar attributes are emphasised and he is merged with various luminal deities and Sun gods. As Baal, the god of the cult would often be simply referred to

The Black Knights

as 'the Lord'. Some have suggested that the rites performed at an Asherah temple would have included a ritualised enactment of the death and resurrection of the Son through the power of the Goddess. Just as it did in the Osirian Mysteries of Isis. This would have easily translated into a Christian context. It should be added of course that no one is suggesting that the Templars, or anyone else, were worshippers of Baal and Astarte. As self declared 'pious Christians' they would have no doubt been outraged by the idea. However many of them do seem to have been interested in the roots of their faith and that faith was undeniably rooted in Roman period paganism. Thus we can only guess what kind of beliefs were in circulation amongst the varied constituents of the Templars. Many of whom had previously been excommunicated and several of whom were, to varying degrees, what we now call 'dual faith observance'. What's more given their secret ambition to be free of the power of the Church, even though under the technical rule of Popes, any 'authentic' Christian sources that differed from orthodoxy would have been very attractive to them. It is also possible, as we shall discover later that this form of Roman 'dual faith' Christo-Paganism had in some form been The Dome of the Rock is also crucial in understanding what the Templars discovered here. The Rock in question is said to be a piece of the original Mount, believed by Muslims to be the site from which Muhammed ascended to heaven. The Dome itself representing the heaven he ascended into, there is thus an interesting parallel with the Holy Sepulchre. In Jewish tradition the Mount and Rock, was the place the World was created from. But inherited by the Templars. The

The Black Knights

main difference being the new emphasise played by the Feminine.

What is even more interesting is what is beneath the mosque. Known for centuries but oddly ignored in most of the popular books on the Templars is something called the Bir el Arweh, or the Well of Souls. This is a small cave directly beneath the Rock, accessible only by a stairway in the mosque. It has the unusual resonant feature of producing oceanic sounds, much like a shell when held to the ear. For Muslims this sound was of the rivers of paradise, said to lie beyond this cave and the cave itself the place in which the dead would congregate on Judgement Day. But the legend is far older and was also know to the Jews as a cave of dead, a place where pre-natal and post-mortem souls prepared for transition and where Elijah, Abraham, David and Solomon meditated and sought contact with another world. As such it was probably the primary secret of the Temple of Jerusalem that once stood here. Probably the Holy of Holies itself. The oldest versions of the myth claim the cave was directly above the Abyss, the chaotic ocean, from which all things emerged and all would return to. The main gate to the Underworld and point of contact with the primeval source. The Templars are not usually linked with this cave but a strange occurrence during the excavations suggests they may have been.

Sometime after the first 1867 exploration one Captain Parker claimed, in a letter dated 1912, to have taken part in further investigations of the tunnels and discovered a secret chamber connected to one of them. This secret chamber led on to another tunnel which rose to the surface where a thin partition was found.

The Black Knights

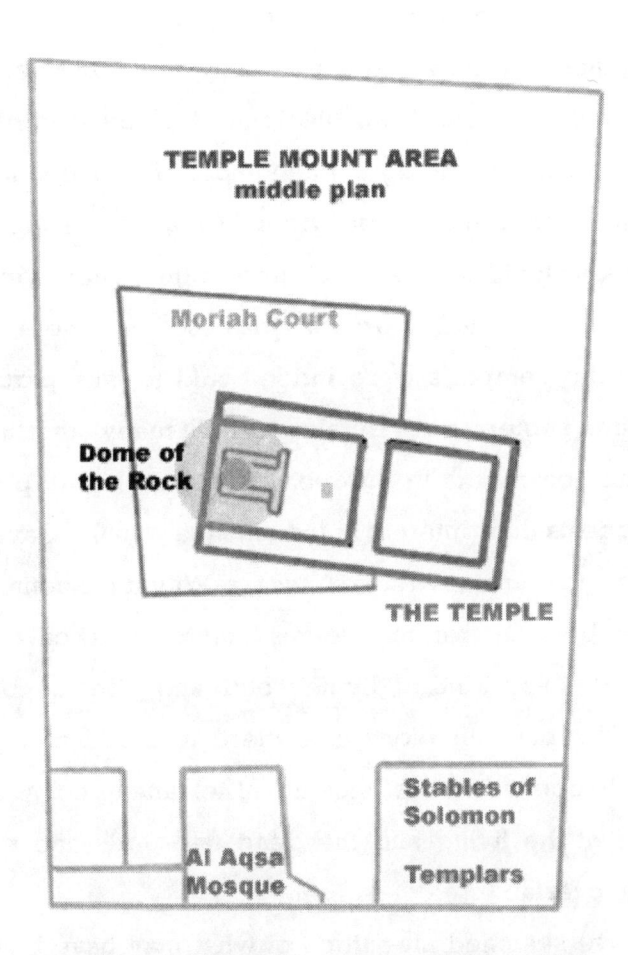

Solomon's First Temple overlaid on the Dome of the Rock (Middle Plan Hypothesis) revealing the Well of Souls directly beneath the Holy of Holies within the First Temple

The Black Knights

On breaking through this partition Parker found himself in the middle of the mosque and was chased off by angry Muslims! If this is a true story it confirms the tunnels as access passages and possible places of ritual. Although now generally regarded as water conduits, sources from the First Crusade describe Jewish inhabitants of the city hiding in them and in the section nearest the Dome of the Rock, a small underground synagogue had been built. The Templars would have known this and their burrowing into the conduits may have had a greater purpose than mere irrigation. Given that the Templars were indeed said to take part in secret nocturnal and subterranean rituals and built many other mysterious underground chambers in Europe, this seems highly plausible. It further suggests their interest in the mosque was the Cave of Souls, to which the conduits gave secret access. Within the context of what has already been suggested it seems likely that this cave may have been regarded as a kind of divine womb and place of contact with the dead. Templar initiations elsewhere would have reproduced what ever happened in this ancient subterranean complex, where the worlds of the living and the dead and gods and men, were believed to overlap.

We thus have sketched an outline of what may have been central to the beliefs of the Templars in the Holy Land. But what occurred there and later in Europe and particularly in England, is also very significant. This where we turn next.

The Black Knights

1 The Abraxian number 365 signified the number of days in a year, seen as the number of solar and planetary orbits, or heavens, around the Earth in a seasonal cycle. Though there is still confusion over whether this mysterious figure represented the worldly presence of their remote Godhead, or their highest evil archon and world ruler. Its ambiguity is akin to that of the Serpent in Ophite theology, a closely related sect, which was certainly always seen as a divine interceder. Some associate Abraxas with the now famous Arabian magical phrase Abrakadabra, Abra Had Abra, or perhaps Abra Ka d'Abra, a spell used in healing, indicating it may have had more benign magical associations. Speculative research has linked 'Abra' with the name 'Abba', Hebrew for 'Father' and the Egyptian god 'Ra'. However astrological magic also often used zoomorphic humanoids in talismans to channel planetary powers, a practise regarded as Diabolic by the Church.

2 Later other bodies of knights attached to the Holy Sepulchre take this name and for a time every knight dubbed in Jerusalem is a 'Knight of the Holy Sepulchre', a prestigious title indicating honorary Crusader status. Many of these knights created local appendent Orders when they returned home. This has muddied the waters for many researchers, but here I am referring to the first knights to be so called and no others.

3 Helen's origin is uncertain, some say she was from the Balkans, but a more common claim is that she was the eldest daughter of a British King, married to a Roman General and Governor. Her child being Constantine, subsequent Governor of Britain and later the Emperor of Rome. It has also been suggested that her Christianity itself was not entirely orthodox, probably the fusion of an early Celtic interpretation of Christianity with Druidism and Native tradition known to have emerged in Britain. This is taken still further by others who point to the fact that Helen was the name of an influential Celtic fertility goddess, who was also the patron of London it is claimed (See the works of *Caroline Wise* for more on this aspect of Helen). There are also resonances with Helen of Troy (another version of the goddess Helen) and the alleged Trojan origins of both the British and Romans. No doubt a Romano-British myth of assimilation. If this Helen was also a sovereignty goddess, then the marriage of the King and her representation in her priestess would have been an important rite, apparently adhered to by the Roman colonists (perhaps observing the Trojan parallels). Constantine's eclecticism may thus have had its roots as much in the late British Mystery Tradition as in Sol Invictus.

Eusebius claimed that before the Battle of Milvian Bridge in 312 AD Constantine saw a cross of light above the Sun and the following night dreamt Christ visited him and informed him that if he converted to Christianity he would be victorious. Other versions of the story have Constantine hearing the words 'in this sign you shall conquer', either at the time of the vision or in the dream.

The Black Knights

Constantine does seem to have marked his armies shields with a cross and did win the battle, eventually becoming Emperor of Rome as a result. However the nature of the cross varies in accounts, some claim it was the Chi-Rho cross, others a Latin cross and yet others an equal armed cross. Most interestingly of all some say the red cross was formed by smears of blood Constantine ordered his men to mark their shields with. However in 308 Constantine had attributed his victory over the Germans to the god Apollo and in 310 claimed a vision of this god in a Solar temple in Gaul. Significantly the equal armed cross and rites of blood were features of the cult of the Sun. But most damning of all, the 'triumphal' Arch of Constantine in Rome is completely devoid of any Christian symbolism, instead showing a figure, apparently Constantine, sacrificing to Silvanus before taking part in bear and boar hunts. Then afterwards sacrificing to Diana, as the god Apollo rises from the sea into the sky. The Sun god is also shown on the eastern side of the arch with the Moon goddess on the western side. In the Edict of Milan made soon after he became Emperor Constantine merely granted freedom to all religions, including his mother's Christianity and only on his deathbed does he convert to the Christian faith. His sons became devout Arian Christians, affirming the mortality of Jesus as a Messianic prophet as much as the divinity of Christ, however he was superseded by his nephews who briefly returned Rome to paganism and persecuted the Christians there.

5 The Church of the Holy Sepulchre is clearly within the walls of Jerusalem and was so in Medieval times. However a few archaeologists claim that this was not the case in Jesus' time and that this is proven by the 1st century graves found around it. But given the position of the church between the Dome on the Rock and David's Tower, both present in some form in the 1st century it can be argued that a position outside of the walls would not be possible.

The Black Knights

Templars Ascendant

The history of the Templars in the Orient over their two centuries is as complex as the politics of the Middle East of the period. Then as now. But generally the Order profited greatly from its spell in the East, both economically and culturally. The bottom line was its financial growth, fostered not only by its attractiveness to donors seeking a place in heaven - or the utilization of a confrater's share in the collective ownership the Order's property - but also by its creation of the first international banking system. Its genius was in its method of transferring the wealth of the Crusaders to and from Palestine. Achieved by issuing a coded letter at their departure point, on receipt of funds and reissuing the same amount on their arrival, minus a fee and interest of course. The funds could be accessed at any Templar 'bank branch' along the way to Palestine and the letter modified accordingly, with a fee added. The client could also overdraw of course, difficult debts were desirable for the Templars, as was the interest they accrued. They had in effect invented the credit card and it made them rich. These ideas were

The Black Knights

not new, similar schemes had been invented by the Byzantines and was operated through their Varangian Guard, while landless Jewish entrepreneurs had refined it. But the Templars deployed it on a far larger scale than anyone before. Their wealth afforded them the most advanced military equipment available and a large force of mercenaries, which, combined with their undeniable 'enthusiasm for battle', made them a formidable and indispensable force in the Crusades.

As their numbers and wealth grew their secular influence spread across the whole of Christendom and their habit of using debt as leverage and other subtle ploys, gave them great political influence and afforded positions of power, though it also led to a corruption that eventually undermined them.

The Templars relationship with the local culture is fairly ambivalent. Most Crusaders adopted local customs to a certain degree. A few went native completely, while others, such as the tyrant Emperor Frederick II rejected Christianity for Arabian science and employed only Saracens at his court in Sicily. Nearly all upper class Europeans born in Palestine were educated locally and learnt Arabic and this was perhaps one of the biggest factor in the subsequent re-civilisation of Europe. On the other hand many of the western Crusading knights were bloodthirsty Christian fundamentalists, responsible for a great many atrocities and acts of intolerance. Things are seldom simply black and white.

The Templars are notable for their position at both extremes of this spectrum. As the Knights of Christ their Rule strictly forbid them

The Black Knights

from the adoption of local custom and they were instructed to maintain a strictly Eurocentric culture in isolation. However this was certainly not the case for their first nine years, when they appear little different from any of the other partly assimilated Crusaders. Moreover, as has been already observed, even after their Rule was adopted this ban seems to have been often ignored.

On the other hand some Templars did follow this Rule quite fanatically and a few appeared quite aggressively Islamophobic. Particularly some of the more zealous Grand Masters, at least two of whom were originally the military Marshals to the Kings of Jerusalem, not known for their tolerance, imposed on the Order by the monarchy When the Templars elected their own leaders more freely the case seems quite different, with the part Syrian Phillip of Nablus being the counter example to the fundamentalists.

A typical example of apparent Templar tolerance can be found in the account of a visiting Saracen official, Usama ibn Mungidh, who was allowed to pray in the mosque in the headquarters of his 'friends and acquaintances' the Templars. When a newly arrived Frankish knight attempted to prevent the Arab, the Templars forcibly ejected the offender from the site instead and guarded the Saracen as he continued his prayer. A more dramatic, though less substantiated, tale has it that when the Knights Hospitallers once chased a fleeing Muslim into the Templar sanctuary, the knights gave him protection and happily fought off their traditional rivals.

But as has observed, we should not forget that other Templars, like most of the Crusaders, sometimes acted in a confusion of religious zealotry and petty personal bias. And as such massacred

The Black Knights

many innocent men, women and children in the region. It is very clearly demonstrated by this kind of dichotomy that the Templars never constituted any kind of homogeneous culture or ethic. The more powerful they became the more corrupt members they attracted and the more often outside powers imposed their favourite candidates in elections.

In their positive dealings with the Arab world the leading Templars were particularly interested in innovation and new philosophies, even more so than other Crusaders, most of whom might today be derided as 'life stylists', or 'fashion victims', in their somewhat shallow adoption of 'Orientalism'. In particular the Templars adopted many practical technologies and methods both directly from the Arab world and indirectly from Byzantium and introduced these to Europe.

They were often criticized for their unusual familiarity with the native population, but whether all these good relations constituted pragmatic diplomacy or ideological exchange is hard to say. They certainly made contact with Arab sects, including the Sufi schools and given what we have so far found regarding their origin, it is highly likely that they were influenced by them. One group they had very close contact with was the Syrian branch of the Ismaili sect of Nazari, popularly known as the Assassins. The Assassins, or Hashashin, were an extreme millennial Shia cult from Persia, organised as a secret society, whose creed could justifiably be described as Islamic Gnosticism. Their favoured political mode of operation was a slow, covert infiltration and manipulation of Muslim

The Black Knights

Caliphates and when necessary an unexpected assassination.[1] The Syrian Assassins differed from their founding chapter in Persia in that they had secretly rejected Islamic law, or Sharia - some claimed even the Koran itself - and allegedly accepted no rule or law, except the commands of their Grand Master, the 'Old Man of the Mountain'. They also seem to have effectively invented the now familiar degree system amongst modern initiatory societies. In which the ancient Mystery grades were modified. In that certain public masks were gradually removed and secrets increasingly revealed, as the initiate rose through the ranks and achieved whatever form of 'enlightenment' was deemed appropriate by their Order.

Many writers have commented on the similarities between the Templars and the Assassins, both in their livery of white and red and in their organisational structures. This seems particularly true after the reforms and organisational changes applied to the Order in 1160 by Bertrand de Blancfort. While this may be coincidence we cannot exclude the possibility of some Ismaili influence on at least one faction within the Templars. Counter indications to this include the famous massacre of the Ismaili envoys, who were seeking an alliance with King of Jerusalem. This attack was carried out by supporters of the former Marshal and then Templar Grand Master, Odo de St Amand in 1173. But the motive for this was apparently concern for the tribute the Assassins were paying the Templars, after their territory was surrounded. The proposed alliance would have repealed this sizeable tribute and lessoned the

The Black Knights

Templar's local income and perhaps their influence over the sect. As we shall see Templar – Assassin alliances seem a crucial factor in the Order's activities as time goes on.

Another area in which oriental culture further effected Crusaders was in the relatively egalitarian gender relations in certain areas. For instance it has been shown that a significant percentage of educators and scholars in the early Islamic period were women. This combined with the example of the likes of Eleanor of Aquitaine seems to have particularly influenced the Templars, who are said to have initiated women into their Order during their early years. No doubt mostly as educators and nuns, a contemporary illustration shows at least one nun in Templar livery. Many of these would probably have been of local origin too. There is evidence that this was the case at least in their first nine years, though after this their Rule specifically ruled out this egalitarian position and banned them from publically associating with women. But even this edict, which clearly stated the Order must 'no longer admit women', is evidence that they initially were. Some claim the custom continued in secret, though this is unlikely. But the Chinon document does indicate the Templars were allowed to meet women in secret and of course most of the secular Templars would have been married.

The full tale of the triumphs and failures of the Templars in the Orient are beyond the scope of this book, but it is important to remember that the Templars reputation largely rested on events in the East. They were not only known for an exemplary chivalry that the medieval 'spin doctors' concocted for them, but also had a

The Black Knights

reputation as a fearsome fighting machine. Largely resting on their beserkir like ferociousness and fanaticism in battle, as much as their tactics and advanced military equipment. A Templar was instructed never to retreat unless vastly out numbered and it is said that at many of their battles even on defeat they showed an eagerness to be martyred and the first to be beheaded.

The Templar expansion in Europe originally consisted of a rich support network to keep the Templar military up and running in Palestine. Acting as an agricultural base, with a large number of farms and mills in its possession, a supplies depot, with its own weapon, wool and linen industries and most importantly a bank. It also used its influence with Kings and Popes to ensure continuing favour for their crusading brothers. It has been recently shown that the majority of Templars away from the battlefront were often quite elderly or infirmed, having little to do but oversee the logistic and business affairs of the Order. The Templars even had a 'retirement home' for the more elderly, infirmed or demented at the island retreat of Temple Denney in Cambridgeshire.

The Order in the west was geared towards supporting the eastern mission. Therefore when the loss of the Holy Land became irrevocable the Order largely lost its reason to exist and many of its leaders lost their way. It was at this point that the naked ambition for power, as well as the more reasonable aspiration for independence, long present in the Order came even more to the fore.

In addition to their fiefdoms across Europe and role in crucial political disputes of the era, the Templars began to look for an

The Black Knights

Ordensland. The concept had been invented by their rivals the German Teutonic Knights, who had colonized much of what would become Prussia, turning it briefly into their own nation. The Templars thus began to look for their own Ordensland, an independent nation that could act as a large scale refuge and a power base in support of its brothers abroad. There were two main candidates for this, Cyprus, championed by the English Templars and the Languedoc, favoured by the French and the Templar Grand Master.

Cyprus had been liberated from tyrannical Byzantine rule by Richard I, who sold it on to his friends in the Templars under Richard de Camville. At this time many Templar supporting nobles moved to the island, including members of the de Vere family, who will become important in our history later. It is likely that the idea of turning this useful supply base into a private Templar nation emerged then. However due to their original view of the island, simply as a base of supplies for the Crusades, with heavy local taxation, while ignoring the concerns of the local population, they soon faced popular revolts. Richard became the dominant power in Palestine on his arrival there and placed his own vassal at the head of the Templars. Soon after this Guy of Lusignan, the then acting ruler of Jerusalem, enthroned by the formerly ruling fundamentalist faction of the Order, was ousted by Richard in favour of Guy's main rival Henry, Count of Champagne – and son of Troubadour loving Marie of Champagne – following the assassination of the only non Templar candidate by the Hashashin. A suitable 'retirement home' was then required for him. It appears

The Black Knights

to have been decided that Cyprus would be it, a place that would also keep him very busy. The Templars thus sold it on to him via Richard. After this, though the Order continued under his protection in Cyprus for some time, following their flight from Palestine, the Templar position here weakened and hopes of it becoming their Ordensland soon faded. Some would later claim that the idea of an overseas 'Ordensland' would remain amongst certain English families well into colonial times, when the Templars were just a dim memory and other associations had taken their place.

The Languedoc in contrast was always a firmer favourite with the French Templars. Largely due to its relative insularity, between the Alps and the Pyrenees and its liberal culture, but also due to the large number of landowners who supported them here. It was also fairly close to Burgundy the homeland of original Templar families. This is also interesting in that Burgundy was said to have been the refuge of the sons of Constantine on their escape from a hostile regime in Rome many centuries before. The exiles supported an Arian form of Christianity and to a certain extent their father's Sol Invictus mythos. It is thus tempting to see both the Cluniacs and their Templar rivals as heirs to an ancient belief system preserved here.[2] Certainly this whole corner of Europe had been the last refuge of Arian Christianity, a heretical branch of the Church who denied the divinity of Christ and also fostered multiple interpretation and toleration by rejecting the concept of heresy. Because of this the region became a refuge for those heretics the

The Black Knights

less tolerant Catholic Church sought to slaughter. Even after this ancient region became officially Catholic it retained its tradition of liberal toleration, becoming the birthplace of Catharism and perhaps even the cult of the Witches Sabbat![3]

The Cathars have long been associated with the Templars. But a direct association is unlikely, as the Cathar priests were devout pacifists and the Templars were anything but. In fact the Templar devotion to John the Baptist is plausibly attributed to the Zealot's toleration of violence, in contrast to the pacifism of Christ. However, as ever things are a little more complex. Catharism as practised covered a broad spectrum of beliefs, ranging from the extreme Gnosticism that has become their public face and triggered their persecution, to a much milder form of Catholic Mysticism, plus all points in between. And including a few sects more akin to the German Brethren of the Free Spirit, which would have a significant influence in proto-Rosicrucian circles. The more conservative end of this spectrum was favoured by the majority of the nobility of this region and these were also often more than a little sympathetic to it's more extreme manifestations. This should come as no surprise, as even a devout Catholic like St Bernard had called the Cathars 'righteous people', declaring 'No sermons are more thoroughly Christian than theirs and their morals are pure', even though he felt they were very misguided in their faith. More liberal Catholics would have rated them even more highly. These same moderate Cathar nobles were also the main financial benefactors of the Templars in this region. Thus it is not hard to see

The Black Knights

the chains of Templar association. It is also possible that one of their most successful Grand Masters, Bertrand de Blancfort, was a relative of the Cathar allied Blanchfort family, one of the most influential in the region. I would suggest it was because of these connections that the Templars refused to take up arms in the Albigensian Crusade and moved most of their forces in the region into neighbouring Aragon. Their excuse being that they did not take part in Crusades in Christian countries, despite doing just that later in other parts of Europe. Curiously however when a troop of knights, taking part in the Crusade under Simon de Montfort, accidentally crossed the border into Aragon, it is recorded that the Templars attacked them and killed many of them, believing it was a deliberate incursion. Perhaps a little too conveniently. It is thus possible that a group of moderate Cathars may have existed within Templar preceptories in the Languedoc and along the Spanish border, but no more than this is likely.

The Templar's 'heretical' association with this region has also been revealed by the secret Chinon documents. In these it clearly emerges that the mysterious 'cult of the head' attributed to the Templars was actually only known in the Montpellier region and therefore was most likely a local phenomena, whose partially understood lore may have spread elsewhere. The preserved heads of saints were common relics in this period, usually those of the decapitated 'martyr' saints, such as John the Baptist, several of whose 'heads' were available on the reliquary market. Curiously the terror evoked in some of the alleged witnesses of these heads is

The Black Knights

reminiscent of the Cluniac rite known as the 'Peace of God', in which troublesome nobles were terrified into a more moral stance by being introduced to the grim physical remnants of saints. On which oaths were pledged and kept at the risk of the saints supernatural vengeance. Given the close origins of the Templars and Cluniacs, it maybe that some Templars had a similar rite.

The region was of course also known for its Black Madonnas, particularly Saint Sara of the Camargue, whose cult appears to have been as important to the Templars as it was to the gypsies of the region. Curiously its rival for the status of Ordenland, Cyprus, was traditionally associated with the cult of Aphrodite, herself a Hellenised local version of Astarte, as was Saint Sara.

If the Templars had not have been suppressed when they were, it is likely that their Ordensland would have emerged in the Languadoc.

This rivalry between the possible locations for an Ordensland may have also reflected the underlying rivalry between English and French Templars. Although of course united under the same Grand Master and originally closely related through common Norman ancestry, the rivalry between the English and French aristocracy made the international nature of the Templars somewhat suspect in both countries. With their national Masters often having to support their own territorial monarchs in order to maintain their toleration. This would often cause rifts within the Order which the Templars

The Black Knights

tried hard to rise above. In addition, Britain had always been regarded as somewhat different, an island off the coast of the Continent, once the sanctuary of Druids from all over Europe and in ancient times associated with the Western Isles of the Dead and Avalon, which later became a kind of Celtic Atlantis.[4] In this respect it is curious that the seal of the English Templars was a mirror image of the Continental seal. Another indication of the strange relationship between English and French Templars is the Cutting of the Elm, mentioned in The Holy Blood and the Holy Grail. This mysterious encounter between Henry II of England and Phillip II of France in 1188, involved a small battle over the fate of an elm tree that Henry had taken shelter under. With the angry French king determined to cut it down, which he eventually did and the English king trying to defend it, before seeking sanctuary in the Templar fortress at Gizors. The authors of the Holy Blood and the Holy Grail imaginatively tied this story into their entertaining theories about the fictitious Priory of Sion. However a far more likely explanation is obvious. In ancient lore the single great tree in a field was the symbol of royalty and only the king had the right to seek shelter under it. Clearly the issue was over Henry's claim to Normandy and the elm a symbol of this. The real significance is the role played by the Templars, on the one hand protecting the English but on the other not assisting them against the French. Such an act would further suspicions on both sides.

The English monarchy was often a great supporter of the Templars and Normandy and Burgundy where its main local allies against the Kingdom of France. No doubt with an eye to their own sovereign

The Black Knights

independence. It was on a visit to Normandy that Hugues de Payen first met Henry I of England and from where he was invited to first visit Britain. We shall now turn to the history of the English Knights Templar, which forms an important pillar of this book.

1 The word 'assassin' is derived from the Hashashin, as it was believed that their agents, often 'sleepers' within the enemy camp, drugged themselves with hashish before performing their often suicidal mission, hence the term Hashashin. Modern Ismailis, of a far less extreme kind, deny this derivation however and postulate rival etymologies. Though it cannot be denied that their ancestors did carry out the clandestine operations attributed to them. But it is also true that their assassinations were highly targeted and never indiscriminate, unlike the civilian massacres carried out by their enemies and indeed most States of the period. The now occasionally heard comparison of the Assassins with modern day right wing Islamist terrorists is thus well wide of the mark.

2 The 'Burgundian Factor' is at the heart of the Templar mystery, as already stated many leadings Templars were from Burgundy and even Hugues de Payens successor, Robert de Craon, a native of Anjou, was referred to in the Order as 'Robert the Burgundian', to emphasise his lineage. Further more when the Templars were arrested in 1307 nearly all those in Burgundy escaped after being tipped off by King Phillip's representatives in the region. Why Burgundy was so important is still unknown, some popular modern writers have suggested it was their close relatedness to the Merovingian Dynasty that was important. This may be the case to a certain extent, as there are curious tales regarding supernatural phenomena, such as stigmata, being associated as much with the certain Burgundians as with their close relatives the Merovingians, perhaps explicable by some kind of 'psychic gene' theory. Maybe. But more important I think was the region's association with heresies such as Arianism. The then Roman Province of what became Medieval Burgundy was the chosen refuge of the sons of Constantine, who were both devout Arians and continuers of their father's semi-pagan religious beliefs. I would suggest that these beliefs had been passed down within the local church, supported by sympathisers amongst certain families in Burgundy and were very important amongst those who formed both the Cluniac Order and the Templars. The Cluniac Order, being the first to form, seemed to inherit the imperial ambitions of the Sol Invictus cult as well as its strange theological totalitarianism. While the Templars though rooted in the same soil and mostly in exile, were a response against this aspect, defending feudal privilege and their own freedom of belief. The

The Black Knights

first schism in the Constantinian foundation perhaps.

3 The research of Carlo Ginzburg, in his book Ecstasies, convincingly indicates that the actual cult that triggered the paranoid fantasies of the Inquisition in the 16th century was a syncretic pagan survival. Probably a hybrid cult from the Scythian Black Sea region, a mix of North Eastern Asiatic Shamanisms, the Dianic and Dionysian Mystery cults of Thrace to the South and Indo-European beliefs from the West. Which was brought with certain Visigoth tribes, via the Hunnish Alps, to the Languedoc. This cult could have been tolerated in this region for centuries, particularly in the mountain regions where the Sabbat was allegedly celebrated.

It is possible that there is even a connection here with the Templars, for not only was the imagery of the wild Roman Diana important in both the Sabbatic cult and Constantine's Sol Invictus, as well as reappearing in tamer form in Templar Marian imagery, but St Denis was also a crucial link. Later the patron saint of France, Saint Denis was originally a popular Bishop of Paris, often conflated with his earlier namesake, the Greek bishop St Dionysius (Denis is the French form of the name). The latter long after his canonisation became a kind of iconic archetype, preserving many of the myths and associations of the Greek god Dionysos. Even the later French mythos of St Denis, his association with vineyard country and his eventual decapitation (and magical talking head!) preserves a Dionysian mythos. As does the names of his constant companions, the priests Eleutheros and Rusticus, exact epithets of Dionysos and Silvanus (or Pan) respectively. Mythically indicating perhaps an Orphic Dionysos (whose avatar Orpheus was similarly decapitated) accompanied by Pan and his more archaic libertine form. Pan himself can arguably be seen as a more traditional Greek aspect of the 'foreign god' Dionysos, stripped of his more controversial Asiatic aspects. Originally a minor goat form god of Arcardian shepherds, this remnant of an ancient horned god became the loyal companion of a closely related Dionysos in the early Bacchic myths, and gradually took on many of the latter's more primal and masculine aspects. Later still the mythographers and poets of the Greek transcendentalist Orphic tradition, reinterpreted him as a more cosmic figure, the 'Great God Pan', just as they had done with their supreme deity, the by then Shiva- like Dionysos.

Saint Denis was also the favourite saint of the Merovingian Dynasty (themselves sometimes said to be of Scythian descent) and through them became patron of the French Royal House, with his shrine their necropolis. But he was also very important to the Templars, who also dedicated some of their churches to him, including at least one in England, at Harewood in Herefordshire (briefly renamed when it was inherited by the Knights of St John). Although there is no strong evidence for it, given what emerges in this book as the most likely secret faith of the Templars, it is tempting to regard this devotion as the 'Christianisation' of a more ancient devotion to Dionysos and his companions with perhaps even a Sabbatic aspect .

The Black Knights

4 There is an interesting development in this mythos. There was a primeval myth in Western Europe that the Setting Sun entered a secret gate to the Underworld on an island in the Western Ocean. This island itself was a magical place on the borders of the Otherworld. In the most ancient times recorded it seems the whole of the British Isles was regarded as such an enchanted island. Hence everything here was often said to mirror the Continent in reverse. As the Isle became more inhabited and better known, Avalon took on the role and the same myths were later transferred to Ireland. After this they were projected further out into the Atlantic, in Classically oriented times merging with Atlantis myths, which fed back to those on the fringe who still thought Britain to be an enchanted island.

The Black Knights

The Templars in England

Hugues de Payen visited Britain in1128. Here as on the Continent he raised men and money for the Order. After 1133 the Templars were granted land by Henry II, or more often donations from generous, local landowners were ratified by him. Initially in Sussex, but more substantially in Essex, where the wealthy Earl de Mandeville was an early patron, along with his close allies Earl Roger de Mowbray and Baron Balliol of East Anglia and Northumbria. Such generosity was often motivated by the availability of the free services of a Templar chaplain, or for regular Templar prayers for the families sanctity and well being. However sometimes the motive seems to have been more subtle. The Templar's first and most important House was built in London, to the west of other early donated land along the banks of the river Fleet, between Holborn and Castle Baynard at Blackfriars, then owned by Baron Fitzrichard. Soon after another House would be

The Black Knights

founded in Scotland at Temple, Midlothian, near Edinburgh.

The story of the Templars in Scotland is highly contentious and before we continue one myth needs to be laid to rest. Many recent publications have made much of the story of Rosslyn Chapel, a mysterious 15th century church built by William Sinclair, Earl of Caithness and Orkney. The chapel appears to not only contain early Masonic symbolism, but also Templar symbols and it is speculated that the Sinclair family protected the Templars in Scotland and foster their continuation in early Freemasonry. Most academics believe this to be nonsense and attribute it to Masonic propaganda of the late 18th and early 19th century, continued by Masonic myth makers ever since. However after an independent examination of the evidence I'm quite convinced that the church does indeed contain esoteric Working Masonic influences if not Speculative Masonic ones. The history of Freemasonry is as complex and contentious as that of the Templars and cannot be fully covered here. But briefly there is much evidence to support the notion that Medieval stone masons, like many craft guilds of the period preserved archaic rituals and esoteric beliefs within their practices. Most guilds 'initiated' members into their craft, but the Stone Masons were slightly different. Travelling around the country from building project to building project required a more verifiable system of professional identification, to ensure good work, safety and a 'closed shop' in their craft. Thus an elaborate system of passwords and secret signs were used amongst them. This along with the religious and socio-political importance of

The Black Knights

architecture also seems to have preserved a high degree of ideology and secret esotericism amongst them. Following the Reformation in England and the end of large scale religious building projects, the majority of Masons looked for work elsewhere and many went to the then still Catholic Kingdom of Scotland. This was almost certainly the skilled workforce used to create amazingly ornate constructions typified by Rosslyn. As in England those most skilled craftsman who directly served the Crown were granted many liberties and called Free Masons.

Soon after this the Masons justified their threatened continuation by opening schools of theoretical Masonry and 'sacred geometry', called Acceptions. For a suitable fee they thus educated the idle but insatiably curious aristocrats of the British Renaissance. People who entered such schools were called the Accepted. Later as secret societies became politically fashionable, the ready-made secret lodges of the 'Free and Accepted Masons' came to be regarded as the ideal cover for such covert political activity. This became particularly popular amongst the Scottish aristocracy. In Jacobean England this would merge itself with the machinations of Francis Bacon to form English Freemasonry.

But where do the Templars fit this story you may ask? The answer is they don't really. As we shall discover in a later chapter Scottish Jacobites were very fond of using an early form of Masonry as the basis for clandestine activity. Later in exile on the Continent various 'Scottish Lodges' emerged that sought a more noble origin to their secret orders than a mere bunch of builders. And so based on the absurd notion that because the Templars employed Masons they

The Black Knights

survived in their Lodges, they began to invent the Templar origins of Freemasonry. The full story is a little more complex but this over simplification will suffice our purposes. Simply put the Rosslyn story and the entire notion of a Templar sanctuary in Scotland that was associated with it, is entirely spurious. A fantasy invented and propagated by elitist Masonry. This does not mean there were no Templars in Scotland or that none ever sought sanctuary there, as this is still a real possibility. Nor does it mean there is no link between Masonry and the Templars, as we shall soon discover. However it does mean that the popular fantasy involving Robert the Bruce and the Sinclairs is total rubbish. The most demonstrable evidence for this is the simple fact that the Sinclair's not only had no connection with the Templars but actually testified against them in the Scottish Trials of 1308. Romantics seeking to enchant their lives with these stories, or feel part of a secret initiatory tradition, will no doubt continue to generate 'explanations' for embarrassing facts like this, but they will remain delusional. Fortunately the truth is mysterious and enchanted enough, so we don't need to dwell here any longer.

The true history of the Templars in Scotland, as of those it Ireland, remains largely unresearched, all we know is a little more land was granted to them in Aberdeenshire in the late 12th century. But of the Templars in England considerably more has been discovered and some of it is quite startling.

As has been described above the first English House of the Templars was founded in London, in fact in Holborn, at the top of

The Black Knights

what is now Chancery Lane. The Templars were here initially granted lands on the banks of the Fleet river, once running to the Thames along what is now Farringdon Road, beneath Holborn Viaduct, formerly the site of a river bridge. As can be imagined from this site today this river was once wide enough to allow small ships to travel inland as far as Holborn and the Templars built at least one dock here. Soon after they established small mills and farms along the banks as well. With the construction of their House further to the West of the Fleet they began to colonize the whole of what is now Holborn. With fettering yards, blacksmiths and armourers established along today's Fetters Lane and a military training ground on the site of what is currently Lincolns Inn Fields along Chancery Lane. But the pride of place went to the Old Temple, their headquarters for the whole of England. Situated in a small private garden lay the first Templar round church in England, modelled on the Holy Sepulchre in Jerusalem and near by it the quarters of the monks, clerics and knights. It is claimed that the site of this Old Temple at Holborn was originally the site of a Roman pagan temple but this has never been confirmed . Later as the Templars grew in England and land was acquired across the country, Holborn Temple became too small and new premises were sought out. In 1184 they transferred to the New Temple, a much larger complex, now housing the Temple Inns of Court on the banks of the Thames. It was here that an even larger round church was built, with a rectangular chancel added in 1231. Chancery Lane was essentially built to connect the Old Temple with the New Temple. The Templars also acquired land on the other bank of

The Black Knights

Thames in Southwark, creating the hundred acre Manor of Paris Gardens, an estate which became amongst the first of London's Liberties, alongside the famous Bankside Liberty of the Clink.1 These riverside properties became very important to the Templars as lying as they did in the Liberties between the City and Westminster and given the exemptions from all tariffs they enjoyed, they were able to monopolize all diplomatic transport along the Thames with their ferry service, giving them privileged access to those in power.

Acquiring the favour of the three Kings Henry, as well as Kings Stephen, Richard and John, the Templars gained many privileges and extensive lands across England, including properties in Hertfordshire (to where the Templar's headquarters was relocated in times of civil war between 1199 and 1254), Essex, Somerset, Lincolnshire, Herefordshire, Gloucestershire, York, Lincolnshire, Oxfordshire, Northamptonshire and Sussex. In addition to those mentioned their early patrons included Earl Robert de Ferrers of Derby, Bernard de Balliol, Baron de Ros and the de Clare family and their relatives the de Veres and Percys. Such land transactions were witnessed and overseen by great Earls, often the Earl of Pembroke. A smaller scale donor whose family would later become very significant was Lady Joan de Grey, who gifted land around Hampton. With vast wealth amassed from such donations and privileges in Europe as well as Britain the Templars funded a large local node of their banking network, which supported and often propped up the Royal Treasury, itself briefly based at the New

The Black Knights

Temple. However the Temple was not always friendly to the Treasury as it was quite common for them to refuse to hand over money entrusted to them by local barons, whose property was confiscated by the Crown. This of course only increased their popularity as a bank for the aristocracy. In addition to hosting large sums of money the Temple was also was a frequent hotel and sometimes permanent residence of Kings and other members of the Royal Family, as well as any visiting Papal legates. At its height the Temple in London also monopolized most of the Royal diplomatic and trading missions

Perhaps the most famous person in England to be closely linked with the Knights Templar is William Marshall. Guillaume Marechal, as he was known in Normandy, was an Anglo-Norman knight renowned for his chivalry and combat skills, as a tournament knight he fought 500 bouts and was said never to have lost a single one. The Archbishop of Canterbury at the time referred to him as 'the greatest knight who ever lived'. He rose to obscurity to become the head of the household security for several English kings, a position also ironically called the Marshal and one of the most powerful men in Europe. His career started as a knight in the service of his uncle the Earl of Salisbury. But they were ambushed by Guy of Lusignan while travelling through France. His uncle was killed and he was taken hostage. Ransomed by Eleanor of Aquitaine he becomes her favourite and in 1170 is appointed as tutor in chivalry to her second son by Henry II. Later in 1182 he was banished from court for 'undue familiarity' with his pupil's wife, Marguerite of France, the

The Black Knights

half sister of Marie of Champagne. Embarking on a Crusade he acquitted himself and vowed to be buried as a Knights Templar. Back in England in 1189 he effectively became the right hand man to King Richard I, who arranged his marriage to 17 year old Isabel de Clare, the richest heiress in England, making him the Earl of Pembroke and giving him large estates in England, Normandy, Wales and Ireland. In 1216 on the death of King John whom he had also served he was elected acting regent of England until the nine year old Henry III came of age. On his death his several sons sequentially inherited his title and estates as well as the role of Marshal of England. William took Templar vows on his deathbed and he and his sons were buried in the Temple church in London. Their stone effigies placed in the centre of the round church. Along with the effigies of Earl de Mandeville of Essex, Baron de Ros of Northumbria and Earl Hugh Bigod of Norfolk and Suffolk, all of whom had been land donors to the Order and in several cases important signatories to the Magna Carta. These families will become very important in our history of the paternalistic English Covenant as it unfolds. That ancient pact between certain influential Normans and Saxons of like-mind and between dual faith nobles and grassroot quasi-pagans.

What is interesting about William Marshall for the subject of this book is the role he played in English Templarism. The richest early backers of the Templars in England were the de Clare family, the most powerful dynasty in England, who as we shall soon discover appear to have been steeped in arcane beliefs. Given the thesis

The Black Knights

that these backers were the real power behind the Templars, the 'Black Knights', it is probably fair to say that the de Clares and specifically the Earls of Pembroke, were the real secret heads of the Order in England. The Templars in most parts of England were rather old, retired figures at the height of the Order, concerned mainly with bureaucracy, but on the Welsh borders and later in Ireland, where they greatly helped the Anglo-Norman colonization, a younger, more martial generation remained throughout their existence. Thus it was here that the real chiefs would have gathered, principally I contend around the Earldom of Pembroke. The marriage of William Marshall into the de Clare family and his inheritance of the Earldom is thus of crucial importance and thus given his power makes him the successor as the true secular Master of the Temple in England. No surprise then that his effigy lies in the pride of place at the centre of the Templar church in London. As we have seen others given this honour were Lord Robert de Ros, a known member of a secular Templar Confraternity and a close relative of the Percy family, Hugh Bigod, a major Templar backer and the Earl of Essex, Geoffrey de Mandeville, a notoriously ruthless baron. All these men were generous patrons of the Templars. But along with other unknown knights, while making up the suggestive number of nine, none are given the same pride of place as William Marshall and his sons. William Marshall's activities are thus very important in our history of the English Templars. He is best known for his support of the Templar friendly monarch Richard I,[2] but his more lasting military achievement was in the continuation of the colonization of Ireland.

The Black Knights

This was begun by the de Clares (after whom County Clare was later named by Lord Sidney) and continued by the Marshalls. In this both were closely assisted by one of their most loyal supporters and kin, the St Leger family. Many of whom permanently settled in Ireland as the local representatives of the Marshals and allied families. Interestingly not only were the St Legers related to the Earls of Pembroke, but were also in-laws of the Hastings family. And it was one of the Hastings family, also kin to the Counts of Champagne, that Hugues de Payen chose as the first official English Master of the Templars. The St Legers would thus seem to have played a middleman role and are indeed recorded as important members of a Templar confraternity.

Arguably the most important role William Marshal played in English history however was in the Baron's Revolt, with his role in facilitating the signing of the Magna Carta. Though a loyal supporter of King John due to his role of Marshal of England, he none the less constantly advised the King to capitulate to the Barons, even while helping him ward off their attacks. Likewise the Templars themselves mostly took a similar stance and sheltered the King within the Temple in London. In contrast most Barons opposed the King, particular those who sponsored the Templars, such as the de Vere and Beaumont families. Even Marshall's own son's, then unrestrained by their future role as Earl Marshals but still Templar confraters, were among the leaders of the Baron's party. Richard Marshall was later declared a traitor by Henry III for his opposition to his French advisors. Thus the Templars and their patrons can be said to have been on both sides of the conflict. While at the same

The Black Knights

time both urging a similar end, eventually manifest as the signing of the Magna Carta at the Temple church in London. The Templars were deploying their typical strategy of playing both sides against the middle. Afterwards William Marshall finally defeated the last recalcitrant Barons, but was criticized for his 'lenient' treatment of them. The end result of all this was a charter of civil liberties for the aristocracy and Church and the legal restraint of the monarch, though this latter element was often ignored.

Later groups such as the Levellers would champion this moment as the enshrining of civil rights for all free English subjects. Giving birth to a law higher than any authority and used this as the basis for their proto libertarian socialism. In addition to supporting the Magna Carta the Templars had also sponsored the founding of the first Baronial Parliament at sites such as Cluniac's Bermondsey Abbey. Thus creating the first seeds of Democracy in England. Later commentators would claim this also represented a return to pre-Norman Anglo-Saxon traditions of participation and rule by consent, rather than might and royal will, as was the case under the early Normans.

This leads us on to another curious element of English Templarism that marked it as a unique, one that I shall call the English Covenant. An apparent survival of a crypto-paganism amongst certain Anglo-Norman families and a revival of Saxon traditions. Again central to this was the de Clare family and their allies.

1. The Liberties were essentially semi autonomous free zones, independent of the laws of the

The Black Knights

City and the other local authorities, under the protectorate of a local landowner with the sanction of the Crown. In the case of Bankside, the Bishop of Winchester and in Paris Gardens, the Knights Templar. They were also the base of legally sanctioned gambling and prostitution and sanctuaries that harboured all manner of heretics and outlaws. Offering a pressure release valve for those under more Draconian rules and a financially useful assimilation of the 'informal economy', they were an important foundation of Medieval England. More information on Bankside and Paris Gardens, together with a thesis on a secret cult allegedly rife within them can be found in book the *Southwark Mysteries* by the visionary poet John Constable.

2. Richard the Lionheart was a favourite of the Templars and amply returned their favours, as well as using the Knights as part of his personal retinue. His popularity may have been due to his Crusading zeal, but also the fact thay he hardly ever set foot in England and so exercised little authority here. The Templars ideal monarch! The Crusades were very important to those remaining in England, as they not only depopulated its criminal element but also distracted monarchs and most of the royal family from their homeland allowing more freedom for the feudal lords (as well as a plentiful supply of 'Crusader widows'). A baron's boomtime!

The Black Knights

Pagan Precursors and the English Covenant

The de Clare family had become wealthy under the patronage of Henry I. Due to their alleged easing of his passage to the throne by removal of the prior monarch, William Rufus, while his elder brother Robert was engaged overseas. The events around this coup are themselves fascinating and perhaps somewhat revealing.

As is well known William Rufus was killed in a 'hunting accident' in the New Forest, when Walter Tyrel shot an arrow into his heart after it missed a stag and glanced off an oak tree. The death served Henry well and in a few days he declared himself king, despite the legitimate chain of succession leading to his brother Robert, who would later concede. Margaret Murray made much of this event, arguing that it represented a pagan king sacrifice in which 'good king' Rufus was a willing participant. Murray's argument is quite fantastical in the main, suggesting the 'pagan Saxons' had

The Black Knights

preserved a sacrificial cycle based on a seven year period activated in dire times - itself based on an eight year dark moon - winter solstice correlation cycle, allegedly governing the sacrifice of ancient Greek kings many centuries earlier. Not only is this historically absurd, it fails to explain why the fanatically anti-Saxon King William II would adopt an Anglo-Saxon custom, particularly when Murray herself claims that the Nordic and Norman, equivalent tradition used a nine year cycle. However while Murray may have been over imaginative in her theory we shouldn't throw the baby out with the bathwater here, as there are some very odd circumstances around this event. The strangest is the account from William of Malmesbury of William's body being found by a forester and charcoal burner, called Perkiss, who carried it on his cart to Winchester, dripping blood on the land all the way. A genuine contemporary account that is also a physical impossibility. But that has echoes both of a sacrificial blood rite and the ancient Germanic custom of ritualistically carrying their chief gods and goddesses across their territory in an open cart. What's more as this happened on August 2nd, during the Lammas festival, a time when in ancient folklore the fertility inducing 'summer corn god' was killed by the death dealing hunter, 'the lord of winter', it is difficult not to conclude something unusual was going on! Also just as a charcoal burner, traditionally regarded as the most ancient of craftsmen - linked with Promethean myths of the discovery of fire and later inspiring a quasi-freemasonry known as the Carbonari – was central to events, their close craft allies the blacksmiths were also implicated in the tale. For according to legend the fleeing

The Black Knights

Tyrel stopped by a stream at a local smithy, to have his horse re-shoed backwards, so as to confuse any pursuers. Another scene that sounds like it came from some Nordic saga. Given their opportune placement, there is an implication that these local craftsmen knew what was going to happen and were assisting the flow of events. Similarly the news of the death travelled unusually fast across Europe and in some cases seemed to be expected. The actual events though mysterious in this way suggest a political conspiracy rather than a pagan sacrifice. Tyrel, the man who fired the fatal shot, leapt on his horse after the deed and escaped to France never to return, without the slightest trouble, despite William being surrounded by a hunting party, who also strangely disperse. When we look closely at this party things become a little clearer though. After Prince Henry seems to have left the scene it is led by Gilbert and Roger de Clare, remote kinsmen to the royal brothers, who with their father had earlier tried to overthrow Rufus in favour of Robert. This same father, Richard de Clare, had a daughter whose husband was none other than Walter Tyrel. With this in mind and the rise of the de Clare family in the reign of Henry I, as well as their friends on the hunt, the Beaumont brothers, things get a little clearer. Similarly the Tyrel family do surprisingly well after this for a family of a regicidal assassin. Members of the family later marrying into the St Leger and d'Arcy families. But what of the mysterious 'pagan' elements?

It is no secret that Rufus, at the very least, had a contempt for Christianity and a lifestyle that could be called 'heathen'. In addition his chief adviser was Randolf Flambard, the son of a

The Black Knights

'witch', as pro-Roman Church chroniclers referred to her. There is little doubt that some form of pagan subculture existed amongst the Normans, many of whose Scandinavian kinsfolk were still openly heathen. They were also moved to witchcraft under the influence of Finnish shamans, who retained their culture till comparatively recent times 1 The Normans themselves were still prone to pagan revivals long into medieval period, with Woden and Thor worship being briefly revived as late as the 10th century by Nordic traditionalists, who rebelled against Duke William Long-sword (931-42). William the Conqueror's father himself was of course known as Robert the Devil for his pagan sympathies. Even late into the reign of Henry I the monarch complained to the Pope that Normandy had returned to paganism again. A powerful pagan subculture clearly existed amongst them. But whether this meant they preserved archaic sacrificial customs is quite another matter!

What does seem to be the case however is that a form of 'dual faith' religion was preserved amongst the indigenous people of these Isles. One closely connected to an earthier 'traditional' wing of the English Church, perhaps through those maintaining a Culdee like faith. But also particularly manifest in the 'pagan' folk customs of the common people. It is important to remember that the religious divisions of this age were more complex than the simplistic Christian vs Pagan account some would have us believe. With between these two extremes a range of dual faith positions, extending from a simple schizoid dual observance religion, to a more camouflaged cult of saints, who were but thin masks for the

The Black Knights

old deities in many cases. The former was particularly true amongst the Saxon yeomanry and Anglo-Celtic peasant communities united under the Norman yoke. While a subculture of Norman and Anglo-Saxon nobles seem to have preserved a near pagan cult of saints within medieval Christianity, tolerated by the English Roman Church. Some of whose influential members were still secretly sympathetic to an English religious culture influenced by the old Celtic Church.

Despite the admitted propaganda against William Rufus from the Church and his popularity with many of the Norman aristocracy, he was not the saint the anti Saxon Murray and Celtic Nationalists, would make him out to be. He was in fact a rather brutal tyrant, like most monarchs of the time, who greatly oppressed the indigenous Anglo-Saxons and the peasant population in general - often ironically with rival Saxon mercenaries. Thus it should come as no surprise that the conspiracy against this well supported tyrant would exploit a broad alliance. One that included not only the political supporters of Henry and Robert, but also all the factions of a Church Rufus reviled and most of the Anglo-Saxon population. The latter did not only include those aristocratic Christian Saxons, still loyal to Edgar the Atheling, and those well placed in the Church, who would in general support Robert, but also those common folk of Hampshire, and the New Forest in particularly, merged into the indigenous population, whose lands had been seized by the Normans as private hunting grounds. A grievaOne interesting individual in this respect is the charcoal burner Perkis -

The Black Knights

whose name derives from the same root as the related "Perkins", "Perkes" and "Purchase" family names, the old Anglo-Saxon word "perch", meaning a small person who dwelt on or near a perch. The family was often described as small and dark, leading some to conclude they were Greek, but more likely indicated an ancestry derived from some assimilated pre-Celtic stock.[2] This ancient family became quite well to do in the area after Henry I's enthronement and so it is likely that they were the ringleaders of the local aspect of this probable conspiracy and perhaps the bearers of an ancient tradition.[3] I would contend that this alliance was the first manifestation of an English Covenant between those of dual faith and toleration that crossed all arbitrary class barriers. One that was also dedicated to the reunification of Norman with the Anglo-Celtic indigenous population, itself long ago integrated at the grassroots level, and the promotion of the best aspects of both cultures within Medieval England. A movement mainstream historians associate with the 'long haired Normans', a generation in England rebelling against their traditionalist parents, and adopting local Saxon customs .

In a conclusion to this brief history it is proposed that the killing of a king was such a psychologically loaded event, linked to deep religious beliefs about the monarchy, that some deeper belief system had to be called on to facilitate it. While a post pagan regicidal tradition is extremely unlikely to have existed in this period, half remembered elements of folklore may have survived and been reconstructed, much as neo-pagans do today, into a

The Black Knights

justifying myth, couched in the aforementioned dual faith of a 'Heathen Christianity' with its semi-pagan grassroots. [4] This I would contend was also an important part of the English Covenant. Thus was created a magical network that entwined the high magick, sorcery and ancient traditions of the nobility, with the 'witchcraft' of the common people. An organic magical bond that did not exist to the same extent anywhere else in Europe at the time. In many ways the Templars may have also sought to serve as a kind of 'occult police' within this network, as part of a more general paternalistic ethos.

After swiftly claiming the throne on the death of Rufus, Henry I and his descendents generously rewarded the de Clares with land and titles and by the 13th century they had obtained vast estates in Wales and 22 English counties, as well as significant colonial possessions in what became County Clare, Ireland. In addition to their ancestral Lordships of Clare in Suffolk and Tonbridge in Kent, they also acquired the hereditary titles of the Earls of Pembroke, the Lords of Glamorgan, the Earls of Hertford, the Earls of Gloucester and various Marcher baronies on the Welsh borders around Hereford. Finally they married into the powerful royal French dynasty of de Clermont, making them one of the most powerful families in Britain – and often even feared by the monarchy itself. King Henry also began the first steps in reuniting the Norman and Anglo-Celtic peoples of England, though often against a common rebellious enemy in Wales and Scotland. Among the chief representatives of the King in this being the de Clares and

The Black Knights

their close relatives the de Veres. Along with their allies and future kin, the Beaumonts in the West and Percys in the North, most of whom had some connection with the fatal Rufus hunt.

One curious phenomena of this English reunification was the Knighten Guild. According to legend West Saxon King Edgar created an Order of thirteen elite knights who served as a royal bodyguard. These were selected on the following conditions - 'Each knight was to be victorious in three trial combats - one above the ground, one under the ground and one in the water; and each knight was, on a given day, to run with spears against all comers in East Smithfield'. William the Conqueror continued the Order -many of his early English infantry being hired Anglo-Saxon and Scandinavian mercenaries - and finally Henry I attached them to the Priory of the Holy Trinity and acquitted them "of all service" in 1115. This mysterious body seems to continue the ancient Nordic tradition of initiatory warrior societies, such as the Joms Vikings or the Berserker, as well as the pagan Saxon Huscarls. Mixed in with some of the initiatory practices of the Mithraic Mysteries. However what little evidence we have indicates they really originate in Norman times and their early history is a myth. It is highly likely that they represented the return of some of those Anglo-Saxon families known to have fled and joined the Byzantine Varangian Guard after the Norman Conquest. That elite bodyguard founded by travelling Scandinavian mercenaries, who we have already found preserved ancient warrior Mysteries. Given this and other similarities between the Knights Templar and the Varangians, the

The Black Knights

Knighten Guild probably represents a visible bridge between these two Orders, as the latter's members returned home.

Thus the Templars also play a crucial role in the reintegration of Saxons into Norman England. Interestingly the Knighten Guild built the church of St Botolph at Aldgate, one of the four churches that stood next to the four original gates of London on the outside of the walls, all of which may have in fact been associated with them at one time. These churches played an esoteric role in the spiritual protection of the City, much like four watchtowers and were the site of observances carried out by those leaving or entering the City for any time.

The northern church of St Botolph's by Bishopsgate was also the site of the trial of the English Templars in 1307, where they were speedily acquitted of all charges. Perhaps the brotherhood of the English Covenant was still as influential then as it had been after 1100.

It could be deduced from the above history that the masterminds behind the plan to put King Henry on the throne were the de Clares. Therefore it is also reasonable to assume it was they who would have exploited the dual faith and 'pagan' elements of Henry's conspiracy. As such it is tempting to place them in the middle of this 'semi-pagan' network. If so they almost certainly would also have been preserving a remnant of the old Culdee religion, a Romanised hybridisation of ancient British Druidry with the first forms of Christianity to arrive on these shores. A faith close to that

The Black Knights

of Constantine's mother, Helen, no doubt, that is often said to have survived on the remote Celtic fringes of Britain. This may sound like pure speculation, however there is a certain amount of good circumstantial evidence behind this intuition. Not least of which is the early integration through inter marriage of the Pembroke family with a branch of the Llewellyn clan during their early implantation in Welsh society. The latter being amongst the traditional supporters of the Welsh Bardic tradition. What's more, following their Welsh adventures the de Clares and Marshalls and their Cambro-Norman supporters, conquered Dublin and Leinster, where they again intermarried locally and eventually became 'more Irish than the Irish', according to many historians. Careful examination of their church dedications in Ireland indicates they appear to have favoured possible remnants of the old Irish Celtic Church found in the cult of the saints.

Before any of this happened however the de Clare family had spent a significant amount of their wealth greatly expanding the Benedictine Priory of St Neots in Cambridgeshire. Their family's founder having earlier rebuilt it and placed it under the patronage of their other family favourite, the ancient Abbey of Bec in Normandy. This apparently prosaic example of religious indulgence is highly suggestive under closer examination. St Neot, whose remains were kept in the Priory after their theft from their old Cornish homeland, was a mysterious 'dwarfish', holy man, who became a monk and priest at Glastonbury and is said to have been an advisor to King Alfred. Later he retired to his native Cornwall

The Black Knights

where he became a hermit and in his subsequent legend demonstrated a mysterious affinity with animals, particularly the stags and birds of the woodlands. He was also said to meditate rather extremely, neck deep in water in a holy well. A pool which also was said to contain three sacred fish, of which he ate one, but no more, at regular intervals. Not surprisingly perhaps he therefore came to be regarded as something of a semi pagan figure and obviously became associated with fishy Celtic mythology, such as the Salmon of Wisdom and other Irish and Cornish folklore elements. He also appears to have become somewhat associated with the more famous St Nicholas from the time of the Priory's re-founding. Who, in addition to the Virgin Mary, was the patron saint of the Norman Abbey of Bec and so the favoured saint of the de Clare family. Interestingly he was also the patron saint of the old Varangian Guard. In fact it could be said that St Neot's was essentially rededicated to St Nicholas and the Virgin Mary, in all but name, with Norman monks from Bec imported to replace English ones. St Nicholas - more famous as the seasonal patron of great feasts, gifts and a benefactor of young children - was also known as the 'Lord of the Seas' in Greece and was the patron of sailors, fishermen and sea creatures, as well as associated with springs and fresh water sources. Many dual faith Greeks therefore associating him with a Christianised Poseidon. It is thus not hard to see the associations that could emerge between the two saints, to whom sacred wells were often also dedicated. Moreover, the legend of St Neot in many respects preserves the surviving folk memory of the Gallic god Nodens. As does the similar earlier

The Black Knights

Cornish Saint Nectan, named after the ancient Irish water god Nechtan, who was also associated with wells, springs and rivers. Nodens was a popular deity found all over Britain and in parts of France, he was a healing and hunting god associated with the processes of life and death, but was associated with subterranean water, sacred springs and wells, the sea, merfolk and things aquatic.

From surviving evidence it appears the Romans thought of him as having three aspects, which they associated with Neptune, Mercury and Mars, as well apparently linking him with the Pan-like Silvanus, Lord of the Wildwoods. Nodens was imported into Ireland as Nuada of the Silver Hand, the first warrior king of the gods (closely associated with Nechtan, possibly his earlier Goidelic form or sub aspect). He was known in Wales as Nudd or Lludd, where his son was the chthonic figure, Gwynn ap Nudd, leader of the ghostly Wild Hunt and ruler over the Fey (aka Alberich to the Normans), who is sometimes modernly thought of as an aspect of his father. It was with these archetypes or god-forms that the Saints Neot, Nectan and Nicholas seem to have become associated with in Britain.

Adding complexity to this hybrid mythology, traditionalist semi-pagans in old Normandy, being of Norse - French descent, would have had a somewhat different take on this. Such dual faith Norsemen would occasionally associate St Nicholas and Nechtan, with the sea daemon Nykur, a chief aquatic spirit of the Vanir sea god Njord and ruler of the elemental Nixies (these old Nordic

The Black Knights

terms, Nykur, Nixies and others, having the same linguistic roots as the Celtic Nechtan etc). Njord himself, the Viking's Neptune, could also have been very easily equated, particularly within the Byzantine Greek influenced Varangian Guard. However they more often associated the the Mercurial aspects of 'St Nicholas' with the late manifestation of shape-shifting Woden, as the second All Father, father of the gods and great ancestor. The earlier All Father of the ancient Nordic tribes and so the father of Woden, was the warlike Tyr, who like Nuada was a bearer of a magical sword and had a single natural hand. Later Tyr was reduced to a simple war god, but I would argue was the original cognate counterpart of 'St Nicholas', through his Nuada / Nodens parallels. It was probably this more aggressive aspect that also made him a patron of the Varangian Guard. Similarly Woden would also be reassigned the role the leadership of the Wild Hunt, from the older Vanir elf god Frey, during Dark Ages. Thus again we have a similar triad of deities Martial, Mercurial and Neptunian, associated with St Nicholas. The fact that these parallels are more than a coincidence is also well evidenced by the confusion in many places between the perceivedly cognate Noden and Woden. Such was the way of ancient multiculturalism, with its hybridized paganisms and dual faith fusions. Old Nicholas thus became the focus for an amalgam of Celto-Nordic folk memories of which much more could be written. [5] But returning from this mythological detour, it is curious that as well as being the much favoured saint of the early Earls of Pembroke and the Norse Varangian Guard, St Nicholas also had an altar in the Temple Church in London, one of the two alongside the high altar,

The Black Knights

the other being dedicated to John the Baptist. It may also be significant that the warlike de Clare's coat of arms consists of three chevels which resemble a triple Tyr rune. Perhaps indicating an origin in a Norman cult of Tyr, that may have grown out of the popular Woden cult, known to be active in Normandy as late as the 12th Century. Such beliefs may have evolved further in Britain and Brittany, in response to contact with similar remnants of the Nodens cult. Given that Nodens was also a God of the Hunt and of Blacksmiths and Foresters, it is possible that any local New Forest 'cabal' would be dedicated to him as well, alongside with other local archetypes [6] and that this would become the 'pagan' point of contact between Norman, Celt and Saxon. Thus on assimilation into British culture the Norman de Clares could have easily made the conversion from what looks like somekind of Viking Voodoo to a unifying Culdee 'cult of the saints', if not a secret British Witchcraft.

As we shall see there is also strong evidence that the Earls of Pembroke have long been central to British Mystery Tradition, along with their close kinsfolk the Beaumonts, de Veres and Percys.[7] All of whom were major supporters of the Templars in England. This close knit cluster of wealthy families, almost one extended family, along with their cadet branches and interrelated allied families, have been continually involved not only with political intrigues and rebellions, but were also constantly found close to the centre of magical and heretically religious circles, throughout British history. I would identify them with the upper reaches of the English Covenant, who in addition to their connection with the evolution of Hermeticism and high culture,

The Black Knights

continued a close relation with grassroots 'witchcraft' circles for many centuries, before modern social changes and divisions eventually pulled them apart.

An Earl of Pembroke, William Herbert, was also central to the controversy around the Shakespeare authorship issue of course, having been an early patron of the bard as well as having the First Folio partly dedicated to him. One of the mysteries around this is the unusual highlighting of the word 'Temple' in the dedication, echoed in the Shakespeare Monument at Westminster Abbey, where the bard's figure points to the same word. The Folio is dedicated both to Pembroke and in a sense to this mysterious 'Temple'. *'It was no fault to approach their Gods, by what meanes they could: And the most, though meanest, of thins are made more precious, when they are dedicated to Temples'.* Perhaps the thesis of this book will shed some light on that particular enigma.

1 In Norman times represented by the 'Witch of Ely', probably sorceress of Finnish origin who famously assisted the Normans against the Saxon Hereward the Wake in the Fens, using the traditional shamanic magic of the Finns.

2 Modern genetic research has shown that the majority of the British population, at least at its grassroots, are predominantly of pre-Celtic origin, with the rest derived from the socially fallen of various incoming races. Former rulers who were later completely absorbed into the ethnic melting pot of Old England, bringing their culture with them. The aristocracy and middle classes, and the dominant culture, are the only factors that have continually changed. Though perhaps some people were considered 'ancient' than others, such as those believed related to the awed forest folk of the Mesolithic period?

3 The later Perkins family was descended from a bailiff and advisor to the 'Wizard' Duke of Gloucester and his sorceress mistress Eleanor Cobham, who himself had sprung from

The Black Knights

a family of servants to the Despensers. Their descendents included Mary (Perkins) Bradbury, one of the Salem witches, as well as the founder of the famous Green Dragon tavern in Boston, thought by some to be a centre for the semi-pagan Dragon Society. It is therefore plausibly believed to have been descended from this Perkis family and to have been a genuine family of 'hereditary witches', or at least the closest to one that ever existed.

4 There is even some indication, quite accurately recorded by Murray, that this may have had some precedent, with the 'murders' of West Saxon Kings Edmund I and Edmund Ironside occurring seventy years (7 x 10) apart, along with the apparent connivance of the Witan in both cases (not withstanding official 'cover stories'). There is even the murder of an earl of royal blood during a hunting expedition by Edmund's son Edgar, fourteen years later (7 x 2) and fifty six years (7 X 8) before the death of Edmund Ironside. William Rufus' death in 1100 occurred eighty four years (7 x 12) after this latter event. This also may explain why a Saxon chronology is used, it may be an appeal to an existing secret Anglo-Saxon history.

5 The name Nodens is thought to mean 'hunter' or 'fisher' and was believed by classical linguist Julius Pokorny to be derived from the Indo-European root *Neu-d from whence also came Nuada and Nudd. But it is not hard to also see the name Neot in there too, which like Nuada was a popular Irish first name, probably derived from the same deity. The ancient Irish water god Nechtan also appears as the Cornish sage St Nectan, who was sometimes compared with the later St Neot. In myth Nechtan was the consort of Bo-ana, a goddess associated with the river Boyne and also sometimes with Bridget, just as was Nuada, clearly identifying the two. Nuada lost his hand in a vicious battle with the leader if the chaotic forces of the Firbolg, just as the Germanic high god Tyr lost his hand in battle with Fenris Wolf. Both these gods were seen as ancient rulers of the gods and symbolised by a sword. They were particular favoured by warriors and probably evolved from an ancient tribal god common to Germanic and Celtic tribes. Nodens begat Gwynn ap Nudd, leader of the Wild Hunt, while Tyr was the first 'father of the gods' before Woden, who himself became the leader of the Wild Hunt in Germanic myth. In both cases father and son could be regarded as closely related god forms if not different aspects of the same power. We have seen how St Nicholas was linked to St Neot, but he too is a patron of the waters like the others and also rides through the sky on a white horse (and much later in a sleigh as Santa Claus), leading his own Wild Hunt. It would thus be amazing if he were NOT considered an incarnation of the Allfather by dual faith Normans.

Brian Branston in his essential *The Lost Gods of England* convincingly argues that the Aesir war god Tyr, or Tiw, is derived from Tiwaz, the ancient Germanic Sky Father and precursor of the concept of the All Father. The later All Father, Wodenaz, being a late comer to the North, who

The Black Knights

absorbed many of the attributes of Tiwaz (as well as a few from the older Vanir god Freyr, the original leader of the Wild Hunt). He also postulates that Njord, sea god and Father of the Vanir gods of Scandinavia, was once a variant of Nerthus, the ancient Earth goddess, ritually carried across the nation in a wagon. Whose gender and form gradually changed within patriarchal, nautical culture. But who later returned as Freya and Frig, consorts to gods Frey and Odin. I would add to this the likelihood the Njord was perhaps not simply a transsexual deity, but actually became an androgene, with male and female aspects, hence becoming the shifting ocean, and later manifesting separately in his children, Frey and Freya, the Lord and Lady. As Njord was said the be the heir of Odin in old Norse lore, much as Horus replaces Osiris, or Dionysos replaces Zeus at the end of an age and that he was the progenitor of the Vanir, he can clearly be regarded as the third All Father, forming a trinity (not unlike the Father, Son and Holy Ghost in some aspects). A trinity which perhaps also correlates with the three ancestors of the Teutonic peoples in Tacitus' Germania, the coast dwelling *Ingaevo* and land locked *Istaevo*, with the inland *Hermio*, at the centre. This would correlate with the three son's of the Norse Adam, Bor, mentioned by Snorri Sturluson as being *Vili*, associated with will and active mind; *Ve*, associated with the senses and passive mind; and the mercurial and vital *Odin*. Who were equated with the biblical Cain, Abel and Seth by dual faith Danes. As an aside we might also mention Henry Lincoln's discovery of the four mysterious round churches on the Danish isle of Bornholm, dedicated to *St Olav* (linked to Odin or Thor), *St Nicholas* (Tyr, Odin or Njord), *St Lawrence* (linked to fertility gods like Frey) and *All Saints* (the church at Nyker). Aligned as one complex, in the shape of the Crow or Raven constellation. Templar symbols were found in the churches.

6 In addition to the Britonnic deity Noden's significance to such a possible folk tradition, we find that the popular Saxon smith god, the wise and chthonic Wayland, was not only the son of a sea goddess and an earlier smith god called Wade, aka the 'Keeper of the Ford' or 'Guardian of the Waters', but also had a warrior, a hunter and an archer for his twin brothers (aspects?). Again revealing parallels with the lore of Nodens, as well as the events in the New Forest. Further ground for syncretic hybridisation, in a nation where Celt and Saxon had long ago fused into a hybrid Anglo-Celtic peasant population in many places. This parallel also mirrors the Noden and All Father trinity fairly closely. We could even trace parallels with the old tradition of Herne the Hunter in nearby Windsor Forest perhaps. While a Romano-Celtic and even Pre-Celtic folklore may have lingered with the common people in some remoter rural areas, the Anglo-Saxon traditions of the earlier culture would have also been extant, particularly amongst yeoman farmers, many of whom were of Saxon descent. These traditions would have been equally absorbed into any eclectic grassroots culture, as no doubt were also Christian and other Biblical themes, such as the tradition of Tubal Cain. Thus other features of the events in the New Forest

The Black Knights

become more significant.

7 It is useful here to give an introductory potted history of these families that will be central to the second half of this book. The Beaumonts accompanied the de Clares on the Rufus Hunt and Gilbert de Clare, 1st Earl Pembroke married Isabel de Beaumont, the daughter of one of the fated huntsmen, Sir Robert de Beaumont, around 1130. He was made Earl of Leicester by Henry I, at the same time his brother became the Earl of Warwick, not long after establishing his rule. These two families would maintain their links through intermarriage. Interestingly the Beaumont family were closely linked to the legends of Robin Hood – along with their alleged pagan associations - as not only were they closely related to its central family, the Earls of Huntington (also related to the de Clares incedently), but traditionally tended the alleged grave of the outlaw at Kirklees Abbey. The real history behind this legend is thought to be the Baron's resistance to King John, that was led by the Beaumonts. The outlaw Robin Hood was a part of this resistance, but he clearly cloaked himself deep within folklore that was far older. See Steve Wilson's excellent *Robin Hood, Spirit of the Forest*, for the mythic apects of this tale, which dovetail closely with the apparent subculture of the English Covenant.

The Percys, were a Norman family from Perci - said to be named after the Persians who settled there in Roman times and/or Perseus, the first Greek hero, absorbed into the Roman Mithraic Mysteries located at Perci and later associated with St George. The name also became associated with Percival of the Arthurian Legends. They arrived with William I and became one of his chief representives in the North of England. The heraldic symbol of the Percys was the triple diamond, perhaps representing a triple Dagaz rune of dawn. The family had a history of esoteric interests culminating with the 9th Earl of Northumberland, Henry Percy, a magician, alchemist and proto scientist, who briefly led the occult 'secret society' known as School of Night. In 1117 Thomas Percy had married Alice de Clare the first of many unions within the same extended family. Branched out gentry members of the Percy Family include Thomas Percy, a Catholic Gunpowder Plot conspirator, linked to Earl Northumberland (a connection strong enough to send Henry to the Tower) and via the related Seymour family, the poet Percy Blysshe Shelley. Ironically the then Earl of Warwick, Robert Rich, kinsman to the Percys, became the chief judicial overseer of the Essex Witch trials, to little effect due to wartime distractions until professional judges were called in. (see *Instruments of Darkness, Witchcraft in England 1550-1750*, by James Sharpe).

Another influential family that intermarried early with the de Clares were the de Vere Earls of Oxford. The de Vere's trace their origin back Normandy, but interestingly use the boar symbol of the House of Flanders as their heraldic symbol (perhaps also refering back to the Elf King Frey, whose totem animal was also the boar). This heraldry was probably due to an important

The Black Knights

marriage into this lineage, which links them to the Flanders – Burgundian clans. [Note - The English de Veres should not be confused with the Veres, or Weres, of Scotland who feature in Nicholas de Vere's imaginative tales of his apparently fascistic 'Imperial Dragon Order'. As this is a completely different lineage!].

In England the progenitor of the family was Earl Auberon de Vere, of Kensington, was considered the inspiration of the legendary Oberon, King of the Fey, due to his alleged descent from Alberich, the Elf King and magical brother of Merovee. Merovee was of course the founder of the now infamous Merovingian line, born of the Germanic Neptune in certain myths, or the god's son the Quinotaur, or Fish-Bull, in others. Even Merovee himself may have originally been a pagan Frankish deity. Just as Minoan King Minos was associated with the chthonic Minotaur in his Labyrinth, the son of a Sea-Bull sent from his father Poseidon. But I don't wish to further popular modern fantasies based on these 'bloodlines'.

The de Vere's also seem to have preserved an ancient Faerie tradition in their manor of Kensington and it was from there in 1115 that Auberon de Vere II, the 1st Earl of Oxford, married Alice de Clare uniting the families and probably merging traditions. The de Vere's subsequently built up a reputation of being the noblest family in the nation, their heraldic symbol being a blazing star, that had appeared above Auberon during the first crusade. The de Veres amassed large amounts of land in southern England, some of which was given to the Abbey of Abingdon, the oldest Saxon Marian monastery in England, with close links to Glastonbury Abbey and with St Helen's nunnery in London. Curiously centuries later Parliamentarian General Fairfax - who had married the ambitious and idealistic 'starry' Anne Vere, a branched out member of the de Vere family, whose father had spent some time in the 'Rosicrucian' Palatinate - returned to Kensington and became its leading dignitary at Holland House. Replacing the executed Royalist Earl of Holland, Henry Rich, a kinsman of Henry Percy, the 'Wizard' Earl of Northumberland and the Warwicks, who had maintained the de Vere tradition there. His daughter Mary Fairfax later married the arch Royalist George Villiers, a descendent of the Beaumonts and another agent of Algenon Percy, 10th Earl of Northumberland (though he appears to have been something of a double agent!). The great networking hub that was Holland House then passed to the Whig Fox family, further key associates of the Northumberland's, involved in political machinations. Holland House was an important networking and ritual site and was probably second only in importance to Syon House, Northumberland's residence, as a centre of political and occult activity. This history becomes very interesting in relation to the so called School of Night, as a possible continuation of the beliefs of Templarism, outlined in the conclusion of this book.A full history of these families and their allies over the past eight centuries would fill many volumes, but a selected history and full genealogy is currently in preparation as a companion booklet to this text.

The Black Knights

The Black Knights

The Heresies and Fall of the Templars

In 1307 disaster befell the Knights Templar, when the fanatical King of France brought charges of heresy against them and ordered their arrest. The causes of this predicament were as complex as history usually is. Popular myth once held that the Vatican was responsible for their downfall, as it was the Pope who ultimately dissolved the Order. But the real instrument of their demise was King Phillip le Bel of France, a greedy megalomaniac deeply in debt to them. However the real force behind this deeply unstable monarch was a rising class of bourgeois bureaucrats in the French court led by Guillaume de Nogaret. A faction who deeply resented the Templars powerful socio-political position, one they desired for themselves. This early manifestation of medieval class conflict between the 'lower' feudal aristocracy and the emerging bourgeoisie was characterised by the characteristic avarice and resentment of the latter and their inversion of former's values and lifestyle. Given his financial situation, it was not difficult for them to

The Black Knights

convince the king of the merits of the Order's suppression and the seizure of their wealth.

It was not the first time this paranoid cabal had targeted it's rivals and opponents for persecution and always the focus was heresy. Typically the charges would include one of 'sexual perversion', then referred to as sodomy, which often, though not always, meant buggery, usually of a ritualistic kind. There usually was also some form of idolatry and/or the denial of the Christian faith involved and vague accusations of malicious witchcraft or evil heathen belief. All designed to attract the attention of the Papal Inquisition, as well as to sanction certain aggressive pious counter measures. Similar charges had been brought both against rival courtiers and outside enemies of the court, ranging from alleged 'witches', at the lower end of the social spectrum, to the Pope himself.[1] These exact charges with some elaboration were levelled against the Templars. The Pope himself was very much under the influence of the French king, having been effectively placed in his position by him and reseated in France, after the fatal demise of his 'heretical' predecessor. At the start of the persecution he refused to believe the charges, perhaps under the influence of his trusted chamberlain, Cardinal Cantelopo, who was very close to the Order. Phillip soon put pressure on him however, leading at one point to his attempted flight from the country. But alas Phillip prevented this and put him under house arrest, totalising his power over him.

The Black Knights

In the case of the Templars there had already been prior claims of strange nocturnal and subterranean rituals, as well as accusations of necromancy. The Order's secrecy further fostered these rumours, as did their reluctance to crusade against the Cathars.

The real coup occurred however when two 'ex Templars' from a Paris jail testified against them. Squin de Flexian had been loyal Prior of a Templar House in the Languedoc, but according to rumour had taken part in a popular insurrection against the French King in Paris in 1305. What followed varies on different tellings. It appears he had been charged with rioting or insurrection, but had made an appeal to Templar Commander Reghellini for a pardon. When this was refused he had acted as if betrayed and together with an associate, the Florentine Noffo Dei, also sometimes said to be a Templar, he had sought out Reghellini's known superior, the Templar Master of Milan, at the Priory of Mount Carmel, apparently seeking redress. When this was denied the two men are said to have assassinated him, a crime for which they were subsequently imprisoned. A third man is sometimes said to have escaped, a ringleader, called the 'Unknown One'. But this may be a later Masonic myth, reproducing the three assassins of Hiram, after they adapted this history for a 'Masonic Templar' rite.

The anti-Semitic Phillip le Bel accused the Jews of being behind the rioting and had them expelled from France, he also accused the Templars of being in league with them and as part of his 'investigation' had Flexian and Dei interviewed. On the promise of release the embittered men were the first to lay serious charges

The Black Knights

against the Templars. These charges included the idolatry of the 'Head of Baphomet' and the denigration of the cross, but in the main accused the Templars of being secretly allied to the Saracens and converts to their beliefs, praising Y'Allah in their secret rituals. Some of this is very interesting but given the circumstances their testimony is hardly reliable. It was used by Phillip as the foundation for the start of his persecution of the Templars and the familiar charges of heresy. Lets examine his charges more closely.

Sexual allegations would not have been hard to level against an all male institution, homosexual practise has always been rife in such situations, whether monastic or military and the Templars were both. What's more their rule banned them from keeping female company and testimony in the Chinon document claims they were privately advised to 'seek out their brothers' if they could not sexually restrain themselves, or find some other secret outlet. There is no sign of any ritualism in this, just the typical sexual frustration - and suppression of any contact with the feminine - required to maintain the aggressiveness of a fighting force. Of course on the other hand most secular Templars were married, a few joined late in life after marriage and others secretly sought the company of prostitutes. A few might even have been celibate! There can be no generalisations about their sexual habits, neither can we even exclude occasional ritual practises. But the general allegations were clearly contrived and no doubt shook some Templars. As would charges of witchcraft. When only a minority of any medieval group would have been practising this.

The Black Knights

Many of the original charges were magnified under torture, with delirious imaginings and random responses adding to the offences and modifying the charges, often in contradictory ways. However two specific charges stand out, one is the Baphomet charge, the other is the Crucifix charge. In the former was a charge of idolatry that combined the 'worship of a head' with the secret idolization of something called Baphomet. The 19th century Occultist Eliphas Levi confused this Baphomet with the mysterious horned gargoyles who appeared on many Templar properties 2, but in reality it was the source of the Templars alleged spiritual power that was referred to. The Inquisitors never discovered what it was, but it was often associated with a preserved head or skull. The mystery remains, but the Templars owned many such heads, most of which were the relics of various saints. The most important one of which seemed to be held in great reverence however. And according to confessions in the Chinon document was associated only with the region of Montpellier. This was Cathar country, a creed which in particular revered John the Baptist. So we need look no further, several such heads were said to be available on the reliquary market.

Why heads were revered at all is more of a puzzle, it might have preserved echoes of a pagan head cult, as some have claimed, though it might have also been influenced by a cult of martyrdom. Templars in the Holy Land were said to have been keen to have become martyrs when captured, which in the hands of the Saracens meant beheading. They also revered saints that had been martyred in this way, such as St John, St Denis and St Catherine. Then again as late as 1572 three people, described as witches and

The Black Knights

sorcerers, stole the decapitated head of the rebel Earl of Northumberland, Thomas Percy (a descendent of that family of Templar patrons) from the spike it had been impaled on following his unsuccessful rebellion. Apparently believing it held magical powers that could be used in future popular uprisings. Thus the truth of the head cult may be found in some dual faith notion involving both these conceptions. Thomas Percy was later beatified as a Catholic martyr.

The Inquisitors wanted to prove Baphomet was a demon whose image the Templars worshipped. In the same way that others had been accused of idolatry for inscribing the name, or image of a spirit, on a talisman that was charged with magical powers. In the early Renaissance magic was popular with many in the aristocracy. But although the image of the former Gnostic Aeon and by then demon, Abraxas, is to be found in talisman-like Templar seals, this charge never stuck. In fact Baphomet was almost certainly a corrupt form of the name Muhammed, indicating some Oriental input, as does the alternative rendition of Abufimat, a Sufi term for 'Father of Wisdom' or 'adept', or the Cabbalistic Atbash decoding of the name as 'Sophia'. All of which point to an Oriental Gnostic conception of an enlightened being, possibly even applicable to Christian martyrs. Perhaps a Baphomet was rather like an ascended master in Theosophy and was a secret dead master of the Order. An interesting further speculation links Baphomet with a term for the devil derived from misconceptions on the identity of Mohammed. [4]

The Black Knights

A charge that seems to have been genuine is that of denouncing or defiling the crucifix. This is still the greatest of all the mysteries of the Templars. Even the Chinon documents seem to confirm that some Templars were taken to one side after their inception into the Order and told to defile the cross or 'reject the crucified one'.[3]
If true the Inquisition would have leapt on this and indeed they did. The Templar defence against it was that it was either a legitimate local rite based on the 'St Peter denial', in which the candidate was supposed to refuse as a test of faith, or at least to avoid true denunciation in some way – as it seems only those who refused were sent to the battlefront - or that this rite had been later used a subterfuge hiding some minority heresy. Probably one secretly introduced into an inner sect of the Order, either by the Templar Master Roncelin de Fos, a Cathar sympathiser, in the early 13th century, or later in that century by Grand Master Thomas Berard, who was accused of introducing unstated 'perverse doctrines' and associating with the Ismaili Assassins. [5] As several researchers have observed, the way these educated Templars described and explored their suspicions sounds like they had actually investigated the claims and believed their sources.

While the fact that the cross was of central importance to most Templars, some of their churches being named after 'the True Cross', supports the idea that this practise must have been a minority one targeted at an important article of faith and therefore comprising strong psychological influence.

Much has been made of the Templars possible links to the Cathars,

The Black Knights

but although this cannot be ruled out it is very unlikely. One reason this is not likely is simply that the Cathar priests were entirely pacifist and did not in any sense support the Crusades. Something hard for a Templar to follow. Cathars also followed a strict lifestyle that would have been immediately apparent if adopted by a monk in a closed community. On the other hand the Templars were sponsored and effectively governed by the local nobility, who in the Languedoc were very sympathetic to the Cathars and sometimes pure Cathars themselves. Despite popular conceptions Catharism was a broad movement, ranging from the extremes of the Albigensian Perfecti to a much more moderate form of Catholic mysticism. It was at this more conservative end of the spectrum that most nobles congregated. During the Albigensian Crusade the Templars refused to take part, but showed no other signs of support. If any form of Catharism entered the Order it would have been little different to the local form of Catholicism that had born them originally. But such Templars may still have sympathised with those more extreme than themselves. The essence of Templar religion was probably not a shared theology, or even a common spirituality, but rather the freedom of their class to believe what they wished and to preserve allied family traditions from outside influences. There may have been a variety of relatively heretical faiths within the vast international order that was the Templars, but a significant Cathar inner group remains extremely unlikely in my opinion.

Finally we have the rumours of strange nocturnal, underground

The Black Knights

rituals and necromancy, or working with the dead. The Templars do seem to have often performed secret rituals, several of which were conducted in crypts. They were also closely associated with underground caverns and tunnels throughout Europe, one of the most interesting being Royston Cave in Hertfordshire.[6] They also faced an unexplained prior charge of necromancy – of working with the spirits of the dead - prior to the trial. All this remains a curious puzzle, until we remember their strange semi-pagan martyr cult and their interest in the sacred cave and tunnels beneath the Temple Mount. These chthonic links and associations with the dead, make things a little clearer. In many ancient Mystery systems the final initiation is just such a subterranean encounter with death. What would be a more fitting fear to overcome for an order of knights?

It always needs to be remembered however that all the 'confessions' extracted from the Templars by their Inquisitors were achieved under torture and often later retracted. This itself is odd as retraction carried a death sentence, while confession led to excommunication. Even in England where torture was illegal, the Master of the Temple refused to confess to the charges, even under promise of release and absolution and eventually died in the Tower of London. This strongly suggests the victims saw themselves as innocent and behaved like the Christian martyrs they believed themselves to be. However not all those who confessed retracted, this is particularly evident in the Chinon documents, where the confessions, particularly regarding the crucifix denunciation, are

The Black Knights

repeated to the Papal investigators under no duress. Some writers point out that this was still under the pain of death if retracted, but given the Templar's love of martyrdom this point just makes things ambiguous. Were those knights who never retracted guilty or mere cowards? Many academics, like Malcolm Barber, believe the latter, but a few continue to doubt it. Alas there is no way to decide between these subjective opinions other than personal intuition.

Further clues can be found when we examine Templar sites. One recently found curiosity regarding the Templar's building projects in London - found by the author while researching local geomancy - casts one esoteric preoccupation of the Templars into sharp focus. This is the precise alignment of the St Pauls ley. But to explain this we need to first briefly examine the mystery of the so called 'ley lines' of popular culture. Discovered by Alfred Watkins in 1921, the 'leys' consist of straight line alignments of churches and other sacred sites, often following the lines of ancient trackways. Popular folklore since the 1960s has it that these are also the channels of mysterious energies, or even pathways of the fey and the dead and much literature has been written on this. Whether this is true or not is far beyond the scope of this exploration, however what does appear to be true is that some of the alignments, perhaps the authentic ones as opposed to the inevitable chance alignments, correspond to the rising and setting of the Sun and Moon and perhaps certain stars, over sacred 'high hills', considered as gateways to the underworld. It has also been suggested by several researchers that the lines consist of ancient ritual procession ways to these sacred hills, along the angle of the appropriate

The Black Knights

astronomical alignments. Such ritual ways would have been initially marked with standing stones and tumuli, with trees or springs on them marked out as sacred. These natural stations were later replaced by pagan shrines, over which churches were later built. Thus an alignment of churches was created apparently accidentally. Curiously however the festivals of saints associated with certain of these churches sometimes corresponds to the day of the sunrise or sunset along the ley line the church was aligned to. Thus indicating that its founders either knew something about these alignments or that the saints days preserved pre-Christian feasts later absorbed by the Church.

The sacred hills of the City of London are Cornhill, the Barbican and most of all its highest point, Ludgate Hill, on which St Paul's Cathedral was built. All of London's true ley lines are orientated to one or more of these. The main alignment of interest for our purposes is that referred to as the St Paul's ley, which passes from the church of St Clement Danes, once used by the Templars, through the Temple round church itself and via the site of the well of St Bride's, onto St Paul's where it follows along the central aisle and onto St Helen's Bishopsgate, first founded by Constantine, before ending at St Dunstan's in Stepney. Amazingly, the physical angle of not only St Paul's aisle, but also the architecture of St Dunstans, St Helens and the Temple chancel orientates exactly to the alignment. What this means is a complex issue, the modern churches were rebuilt and orientated by Christopher Wren and his assistant the Nicholas Hawksmoor, both of whom may have been

The Black Knights

aware of such alignments. However their foundations, which could have shared the same alignments, mostly date to the early 13th century, with at least one church built by the Templars, one used by them and another, a rebuilding of St Helen's, associated with what may have been their ancient spiritual ancestry. It is thus possible that a prior alignment may date to the Roman period, or even earlier. But the real mystery begins when we calculate what astronomical event was marked by the Templar alignment and find that whereas others are obvious events - such as the sunrise at the Spring Equinox that occurs between St Paul's Cross and St Michael's Cornhill - this orientates to the sunrise of April 3rd. The only significant Christian festival on this date is the feast of St Mary of Egypt, or 'Mary Gip', a reformed prostitute archetype often wrongly identified with Mary Magdalene in the Middle Ages. This is curious because this St Mary also appears prominently on a stained glass window of Chartres Cathedral, immediately above a crypt which many claim the Templars used for their initiations. Her presence there has always been something of a puzzle. Even more curious is the fact that this Saints day was moved by the Roman Church from its previous earlier date in the Orthodox calendar for no apparent reason. But doing so caused it to coincide with an important Roman pagan festival, the rising of the Queen of Hades, Proserpina, from the Underworld. It was also the feast of Bona Dea, a more benign deity sometimes regarded as an aspect of Aphrodite, the polar opposite of Proserpina (Greek Persephone), who in some myths descended as she rose and vice versa. The two deities often regarded in the Orient as the twin aspects of an

The Black Knights

ambivalent Astarte. In the pagan world this day was also the eve of the festival of Magna Mater, or Cybele, on April 4th. All this may be highly significant as a close reading of the legend of Mary of Egypt - initially an Egyptian seductress who waylaid Christian pilgrims in Jerusalem, before converting under the influence of the Virgin Mary at the Holy Sepulchre - reveals not only the echoes of the mythos of Aphrodite and Persephone, as observed by Robert Graves, but also in her later life of Lilith too, in her role as a naked, desert hermit in emulation of the cult of John the Baptist. This might all be coincidence were it not for the obvious points of Templar interest and the curious pomegranates carved on the outer pillars the Temple church, the symbols not only of the Virgin Mary, to whom the church is officially dedicated, but also of Persephone and Demeter as well. Something very odd is clearly indicated here, especially when we recall the identification of the 'St Catherine' of Royston with Persephone, as well as the possible Venus / Astarte / Asherah links identified at the Holy Sepulchre in Jerusalem. Perhaps the Templars interest in the Languedoc, with its many Black Madonnas, is significant in this respect and their occupation of Cyprus, former cult centre for Astarte and her Greek incarnation Aphrodite, was more than just a strategic one after all?

This is not to say that the Templars were secret cultists of Astarte of course, this would strain credulity a little too far, but what it does seem to indicate is that the original Templar version of Christianity was a very ancient one. It had not only preserved pagan images and motifs within its dual faith cult of saints, as had many medieval

The Black Knights

sects, but that also preserved certain pagan practises in a Christian guise. One of which included a subterranean descent into and return from the underworld land of the dead. Usually this occurred under the patronage of a dark feminine power, that was often identified with Mary Gip and the Black Madonna. This probably originated with Emperor Constantine's first paganised Christianity, modelled on the Sol Invictus Cult, with subsequent additions and modifications over subsequent centuries, such as the ethos of the Celtic Church and influences from the Orient. The last of which was the renewed emphasis on the 'Divine Feminine' brought back to Europe from Moorish Spain via the Troubadours and from the East by the Crusaders. This eclectic mix however would have still have been regarded by most of these early 12th century Templars as devoutly Christian and perfectly compatible with the Catholic faith. This may have been less the case in Norman and other Nordic domains however, where the Old Religion died hard and the Christian veneer of the local Templarism may have been much thinner. By the late 13th Century though, outside of perhaps small, private circles, this old tradition would have become considerably moderated, even in England, with the majority of Templars little different to orthodox Catholics. Something not of importance to those using them as a well established private militia.

Returning to the fall of the Templars it is not hard to see how these irregularities could have been exploited by the Order's enemies and turned into trumped up charges. Most of the Templars would have genuinely denied these charges, being forced to confess only

The Black Knights

by most extreme torture. Outside France, were King Phillip had installed his own compliment Pope, Clement, having ousted Boniface, this Inquisitional torture was far lighter. In England were confessional torture was illegal, it was only briefly allowed by King Edward and his investigators, interrogating Templar 'detainees' in the Tower, for the visiting Inquisitors from France, under Cluniac Abbot Deodatus, but only if no disfigurement, maiming or great blood loss occurred, an interesting insight on French practise. Here, as in Spain where no torture occurred, confessions were much harder to achieve. In England and Scotland, little was obtained at all outside of some obviously forced claims and the 'total confession' of Treasurer John Stokes obtained under duress.

However there were in circulation some other interesting claims and rumours which would surface at the trial. The most famous being the allegations of a 'wild' prostitute of St Giles called Agnes Lovecata. This woman recounted tales told to her by friends of secret rituals and Baphometic idols at Temple Dinsley, in Hertford, thus conveniently echoing the French confessions. The most interesting though was reported by John de Eure, who claimed the Templar Preceptor of Temple Westerdale, in Yorkshire, William de la Fenne, had once dined with him and his wife. At this meeting the Templar was said to have shown Lady de Eure a book, in which she found a paper affirming an 'anti Christian heresy'. The Templar then took the book back and explained the paper was just a 'great ribald'. They were subsequently informed by Frater William, another Templar from Faxfleet, that the Preceptor was a layman rather than a monk and so had no understanding of what the book

The Black Knights

contained! The book or paper was never found. Faxfleet Preceptory would achieve fame as harbouring the largest number of arrested Templars in Yorkshire. Yorkshire Templars may have been fond of ribaldry, as we hear from John de Nassington that Templar Confraters Sir Miles Stapledon and Adam Everingham had told him that at a great feast at Temple Hirst, the knights were accustomed to worshipping a calf at this occasion, travelling there from all over England! Stapledon and Everingham were given Temple Hirst by the King after the Order was dissolved. While in neighbouring Ribston, Augustine Friar Robert de Oteringham reported that he had been spooked by the strange activity and lights that burned all night in the Templar chapel, whose occupants told him 'relics were being unpacked'. When he queried why an altar cross appeared to have been thrown down in the chapel he was told to keep silent. More worldly complaints came from Somerset where the Templars were accused of seizing legal seals in order to grant themselves land 'wherever they pleased'. None of these claims were substantiated. Most of the charges of cross denial were curiously targeted at Templars based in Southwark (probably Paris Gardens), the Knights here abjured the charges and were absolved, but never further commented on their guilt or innocence.

However Ireland was slightly more productive, here a friar called Roger claimed that Master of the Temple Brother Henry Danet owed his position to having slept with the Grand Master in Cyprus. Danet perhaps aggrieved at the lack of support from his brothers

The Black Knights

on this proceeded to make his own allegations. He claimed that the Templar Commander of the Castle of Athlit near Haifa had denied Christ and asked his brothers to do the same on initiation and that Brother Hugh of Ampurias had become a Muslim. He also said that certain Spanish Templars in Cyprus had denied the sacraments. All of which could indicate a denial of the divinity of Christ under Islamic influence. He denied all knowledge of the other charges, but said he'd heard that a Templar in Northern Spain had a head that answered questions. Either indicating a local magical interest or throwing more light on the 'Baphomet' head.

The Templars in Britain were better treated due to King Edward's sympathy for them. Most were simply absolved and pensioned off to join other orders after the Pope finally dissolved the Templars in 1312, following five years of investigation and trial. The rare exceptions being the English Templar Master who died in the Tower and a particularly nasty persecution of Templars in Bristol. Many Templars also seem to have continued as such for quite a while on the countries fringes, with records of Templar burials in the West Country up until the mid 14th Century. While Templar property mainly passed to the Knights of St John.

On the Continent their fate was mixed, some kingdoms, notably those of Spain and Portugal, along with other Latin regions, there was even more leniency than in England, where many simply quietly transferred to new Orders, such as the Knights of Christ. In Germany a harsh fate was perhaps discussed for the Templars

The Black Knights

during a special Church assembly in Mainz on 11 May 1310, until the Templar Master of Germany, Hugo of Gumbach, led a group of knights in full armour against the assembled Council. Challenging their accusers to trial by combat the charges were swiftly dropped. Later however they were dissolved here with the rest of the Order. In France and its dominions the story was very different of course with the eventual mass execution of Templars who recanted their confessions, including finally the Grand Master himself. But even here there were a few oddities, such as the 'tip off' that led to the flight of every Templar in Burgundy before the arrests. However these incidents, which even included a possible aborted Templar coup attempt in Burgundy, were exceptions to the rule, that saw the complete suppression of the Order. The till recently secret Chinon document shows the Pope absolved the Order, privately regarding it as innocent of all the charges. But it was felt the Order's reputation had been so tarnished that dissolution was the only option left, for an Order styled as the exemplar of Christian chivalry!

Some have suggested that an inner Order of Templars, perhaps the Burgundians, self destructed their own Order due to its obvious corruption and escaped somewhere, but this is extremely unlikely. The Templars had certainly strayed from their original intentions, lost their purpose with the fall of Palestine and degenerated into just another Medieval power bloc, in many ways the first international Corporation. It is possible though that if there was a secret subgroup behind the crucifix rite that this was an attempt to reform or reinvent an order which seemed to have lost its way. In

The Black Knights

its last years the Order was something of a fossilised institution full of ageing bureaucrats and power hungry autocrats. An attempt to revive it from a covert cell inside the Order would have been an intelligent move. And while most Templars were the uneducated fighting men many sources reveal them as, including even their last Grand Master, the Templar trial revealed a very savvy and well educated sector of lawyers and diplomats within the Order, quite capable of contingency planning. As were the barons funding and directing them. However the Templars never had the power to influence the reactionary whims of the French court and so alas such an enticing conspiracy theory, like all such Romanticisms have ultimately to be rejected.

On the other hand before throwing the baby out with the bathwater, the idea of a reformist inner group is quite plausible. Most monastic groups have historically developed their own reformist wing, which eventually breaks away and forms a new order, this happens later within the Cistercian Order, which gives birth to the Trappists. Any Templar version of this process would have been particularly secret no doubt given their known modus operandi. Do we have any real indication that this may have occurred within the Order though?

As we've seen, some of the Templars blamed the 'crucifix denial' on the heretical ideas brought into the Order after 1250 by Thomas Berard, who they suspected of dalliance with the Ismaili Assassins. As I don't find the 'Rite of St Peter' explanation a plausible one and have already demonstrated why the Cathar explanation is unlikely,

The Black Knights

I tend to find this charge very credible. The much touted structural similarities between the Templars and the Assassins after the mid 12th century their development under Grand Master Bertrand de Blancfort are very interesting in this respect 2. As are the probable conspiratorial connections between them a few decades later in the time of Richard the Lionheart. These at least indicate an interest in and alliance with the powerful Ismaili secret society, one that Berard himself seemed to have later exploited in an assassination plot against King Edward.4 This would not really be surprising if as it appears the Templar's founders were already influenced by secret Ismaili ideas introduced from Moorish Spain, both directly via the de Payen family, as well as indirectly via the Troubadours of Aquitaine and Champagne. There have also long been claims that they were in contact with other Ismaili, or Ismaili influenced groups, as soon as they arrived in Palestine, the usual candidates, apart from the Assassins and Sufis, being the Druze, the Yezidis and perhaps the Mandaeans. Early in their history the Templars had also established a rapport with the Fatamid Dynasty by capturing an assassin of one of their Caliphs in Ascalon and sending him back to them for a ransom. So all the links are there.

We have no idea what 'perverse' doctrines Berard might have introduced into the Order, he seems to have spent most of his adult life in Palestine and to have been much preoccupied with the imminent collapse of the Crusader kingdom. All we know is that he had become close to the Teutonic Knights and was desperately seeking assistance and other alliances. But we can make educated guesses. While we can trace a Sufi influenced, quasi-pagan, dual

The Black Knights

faith Catholicism throughout the existence of the Knights Templars, there are other irregularities that don't quite fit this pattern. We might dub these the 'Baphomet factor', where, although being derived from the name Muhammed, the term 'Baphomet' is used in a way that seems to signify a kind of Islamic Gnosis, given the linguistic puns deliberately evoked by it. The initiate becomes a 'Muhammed', just as the true Christian mystic becomes a 'Christ' and the Buddhist becomes a 'Buddha'. There are also Brother Danet's claims that seem to indicate the emergence of a distinctly Islamic Christology. All of which seem to be a late development. Given that the inner teachings of the Syrian Ismailis, as far as we know them, appear to have involved the progressive initiatory denial of established faith, an origin of the Baphometic elements in the system of the Hashashin seems very plausible. Reformist groups tend to react against corruption by seeking out their roots and then intensifying them. While the aim of the Syrian Hashashin, according to their most radical interpreters, was the ascent into a nihilistic state of enlightenment, in which all faith was finally put solely into their Messianic Imam who manifested the 'Will of Allah'. Eventually the initiate might become the leader of his own local chapter and himself become the focus of this devotion. In essence this is a corrupted version of the Persian Sufi and Ismaili theology found in texts such as the Conversation of the Birds, where a great spiritual quest is undertaken leading to the realisation of the searcher's own divinity. Now while it seems unlikely, to say the least, that the Templars really became western Hashashin, or Ismaili Sufi mystics, it does seem plausible that some of them were

The Black Knights

initiated into this tradition. In fact we know at least one, Brother Montband, actually was and that a faction of them may have adopted a no doubt very Christianised version of this belief system. Drawing on their own foundational beliefs in the process. It has been claimed that on creating their own chapter the Hashashin adept was charged with creating their own belief system leading to the desired nihilistic epiphany. 'Nothing is true everything is permitted', as William Burroughs wrongly put into the mouth of Hasan e Sabah, the Hashashin's Persian founder. An imaginative fantasy, but perhaps one closer to the truth than even he realised.

One likely first base for this reformist faction would have been the impregnable Templar castle of Athlit, in Syrian Galilee close to Haifa. Guarding the road to a large Carmelite Abbey devoted to St Catherine. As we have seen Brother Danet identified an irregular form of initiation here, involving the denial of Christ. It was also a site long associated with mysterious activities, due to its deep impregnable defences and near complete isolation on a small sea girt peninsula. Only Templars were allowed into its inner walls, which had been successfully defended from all attacks not only by the Saracens, but also Christian enemies, such as Frederick II. It is also famous for having the only round Holy Sepulchre church within a Templar complex in Palestine, the other two being in England and Portugal. Built in 1218, as a joint effort between the Knights Templar and the Teutonic Knights, with the assistance of the French, the castle became an important centre for alliances and pacts between these founding parties. Curiously it was built on the

The Black Knights

foundations of an old Phoenician fortress and some of its ancient walls were used in the castle's construction. Phoenician artefacts were also found here by the Templars during construction, which according to modern archaeology would have revealed the site as a defended port and a cult site of Baal Melkart, the sea god Yam and an Isis like goddess. By 1290 it was solely Templar and the last of the well defended fortresses in Palestine, with a semi autonomous Templar village protected within its outer walls. When Christian Palestine was overrun in 1291 Athlit was still a secure fortress, but has to be abandoned given the broader strategic situation. The Order decamped to Sidon, from were it left for Cyprus and eventually returned home. The importance of Athlit in these last days and its proximity to the territory held by the Hashashin north of Haifa, make it the most likely origin of any Baphometic faction. All of this remains speculative of course and much more research is required in this area, but a likely pattern can be detected here.

After their final return home in the early 14th century and their refocusing on European affairs, the Templars brought more new innovations, but would soon meet their fate. However some claim they did not end here. It is to this matter we now turn.

1 Although the Pope concerned, Boniface VIII, whose notorious libertine lifestyle allegedly left him 'two eyes in a wasted body', had earlier described sex as 'of no more significance than the rubbing one's hands together'. So may not have been exactly innocent! His support for the earliest stirrings of the Renaissance in Rome, also led to charges of idolatry and planetary image magic.

The Black Knights

2 The bare breasted, horned and winged demons sitting in a strange squat, in some way recall an androgynous Cernunnos, with the addition of bats wings, indicating their demonic status. They were never objects of veneration however and if they had any purpose other than decoration, they were at best guardians of the building and at worst the Templar conception of the devil as the agent of a vengeful and protective God. If any Templars adopted Sabbatic practise this image would have been a natural one to venerate of course.

3 The Chinon documents reveal a risible defence by confessed knights that they were forced to spit on the cross and denounce it by their initiator, who had taken them to one side after the other brothers had left. Most claimed they had refused despite all encouragement to do so and even those who complied claimed to have done so under duress but not with their true heart. Many claimed to have been offended by the rite and to have desired reform to the Order because of it. Thus allowing their absolution while confirming the rite. The mainstream, conservative interpretation of this is that as a retraction of a confession would have led to death this was their only option. However Templars were unlikely to have been that rational and the keenness to martyrdom shown by their more orthodox brothers would indicate death was not a great deterrent to them. This may not have been seen as an issue that merited it of course, perhaps denouncing the Order and other brothers was seen as more palatable than self damnation. But further indication that this accusation was accepted comes from the Templar defence lawyers, the language of whose testimony implies informal investigations into this practise had already occurred and included an explanation of its possible use in some houses (see main text). An option in other cases for executed Templars to take a similar line, at no risk to anyone, was oddly never taken. The issue remains unresolved, but intuitively there is a little fire within all this smoke, particularly in light of the irregularities of the Order and is strange secrecy.

4 The derivation of the Provencal word Bafometz is almost certainly from the Spanish form of Mohamet, Mafomet. However Christians often regarded Mohammed as the devil incarnate, or the anti-Christ, thus similar names such as Mahound came to mean the devil. An interpretation that perfectly fits the use of the term Baphomet in both Troubadour and Inquisitional sources.

5 Berard was famous for two things forming an alliance with the Teutonic Knights and ending rivalry with the Hospitallers and saving King Edward from death at the hands of a killer sent by the Assassins. The first was a move of necessity given immanent invasion by Mameluks from the south and Mongols from the north. Certain ideas adopted from these rival Orders appear within the Templars at this time. After King Edward was stabbed by the poisoned knife of an

The Black Knights

Assassin, but survived, Berard was also at hand to administer the antidote, probably calabar bean which negates atropine poisoning. A few years earlier Edward had ransacked the Temple in London after the Templars were seen as too close to the Barons. Some see in this a parallel with the assassination of Conrad almost a century earlier by Assassins, hired by Templars, working for Richard I. It is thus suggested he allied with more than just Crusader Orders.

6 Royston Cave is a curious underground chamber beneath a crossroads by Templar property in Hertfordshire. Graffiti on its walls is similar that found on Templar prison walls at Chinon, featuring Christian, Pagan and mystical imagery. Most prominent, apart from a Crucifixion scene, is a giant St Christopher sporting a massive erect phallus, probably the 'opener of the way' in any ritual (In Egypt St Christopher was portrayed dog headed like Anubis). There is also a sinister looking St Catherine, with her wheel, who has been compared with Fortuna, a Wyrd Sister and Persephone. The latter particularly interesting for a chthonic rite, as Mistress of Hades and the Dead. Images of Persephone which precisely match the cave picture have been found on Orphic and other Hellenic vases. The age of the graffiti is unknown however. It is tempting to equate this both with the Well of Souls under the Dome on the Rock and the legendary Resurrection cave of the Holy Sepulchre in Jerusalem. The cave at Royston is also said to have once had a stone over its entrance, as effectively did the Well of Souls, both stones being regarded by some as seals to the Underworld. Royston Cave's oldest known custodian was a member of the de Vere family.

The Black Knights

Royston's St Catherine   Greek Persephone

The Black Knights

Templar Survivals, Real and Imaginary

The notion of the secret survival of the Templars goes back at least to the late 18th century and probably before. The common claim being that they were in some way the ancestors of the Freemasons. This Romantic idea like most is pure fantasy, though as we have seen throughout this exploration there is rarely smoke without fire. But first we must dispel a few of the myths that have muddied the waters.

The best known story is that the Templars escaped France with their treasure and sought sanctuary in Scotland, where they then helped Robert the Bruce defeat the English. These Templar exiles then survived as a secret Order of the Temple, under the Sinclair family, which had built Rosslyn Chapel. This group is said to have eventually evolved into ancient Scottish Freemasonry. Spurious

The Black Knights

links between the Knights Templar and the Freemasons are often deployed to support this theory. Earlier it was shown how Rosslyn had no connections with the Templars at all and more plausible origins of the cult of Freemasonry were given. This is further supported by the fact that the leading member of the Sinclair family at the time of the trials actually gave evidence against the Templars. Claiming the local Scottish Templar commander he knew seemed a decent chap, but he was unsure of some of the others. The counter claim that this may have represented a schism in the Order isn't really plausible, as those carrying out the trials would hardly have overlooked this. Nor is it likely that Sinclair represented one of the Black Knights, as one person who did, if anyone did, the last de Clare Earl of Gloucester, who died fighting against Robert the Bruce. This raises the even stronger objection, that neither the Templars themselves or their backers were fugitives in England, as King Edward had long been a supporter of them and only ever reluctantly and half heartedly moved against them. The truth about this Masonic claim is that it dates back to the Jacobite rebellion and those exiled Stuart supporters in France who were enmeshed in early Freemasonry. The aristocratic lodges that originally sheltered and supported them were operating alongside a host of aloof neo-chivalric orders within Continental Royalist circles and this, together no doubt with a certain snobbishness, made the idea that Ancient Freemasonry had descended via the Knights Templar, or some other chivalric body, rather than their building contractors, very attractive and it was soon enthusiastically adopted. This idea later spread meme-like

The Black Knights

throughout aristocratic Freemasonry across Europe, evolving a supporting 'history' and body of 'evidence' as it went. The rest is history as they say. The myth is today actively promoted by certain inner orders of Modern Freemasonry, who still style themselves as Templars, as well Neo-Templar groups who followed in their wake.

One infamous document associated with this mythology is the Larmenius charter. This document was produced by one Fabre-Palaprat in 1808 in support of his own chivalric, occult society, the New Order of the Temple, which in turn was connected to this Neo-Gnostic Johannite Church, based on an unusual version of the Gospel Of John. Both these texts are now universally recognised by scholars as forgeries. The infamous Larmenius charter proported to be a genuine Templar document listing the 'secret Grand Masters' of the Order from their last historical leader, Jacques de Molay, to the Duc of Orleans, and onwards of course to Fabre-Palaprat. As such it also chartered the public revival of the Order. The society was loosely connected to French Freemasonry but styled itself as an independent chivalric body. It only lasted until 1840, but it provided the first seed from which emerged what we know today as the Neo-Gnostic Church and its schisms, and through this the original Ordo Templi Orientis (OTO).[1]

More significantly nearly all the current 'Knights Templar' orders use the Larmenius charter as proof of their 'authenticity', as do several of the inner Masonic orders. Many of these now deluding well placed and influential members of the Establishment. Fabre-Palaprat also drew on the Scottish Templar meme in his mythos,

The Black Knights

and the fact that his fake lineage included the Duc de Orleans may be telling. There is some evidenced Orleans was using a form of Scottish or Templar Masonry as an instrument in his own much documented conspiratorial activities during the French Revolution. After he had been expelled from the then conservative Grand Orient of French Freemasonry, for which he had previously served as Grand Master. It is even claimed he had the sword of Jacques de Molay in his possession, a tool used by Fabre-Palaprat two decades later. Given that Fabre-Palaprat's order initially had the public backing of the Napoleanic government, some of his material may have been passed down by way of fringe Templar lodges, such as those of d'Orleans, which tended to support moderate 'revolutionary' factions, after having evolved from insurrectionary Jacobite origins.[2]

But things are a little more complex than this basic sceptical position would suggest, for while the claims of the likes of Fabre-Palaprat are obvious fantasies ,there remains something mysterious beneath the surface. For instance Chevalier Ramsey, the first Jacobite spokesperson to articulate the chivalric origins of Freemasonry (though not its Templar origins), was the secretary of the writer and churchman, Francois Fenelon, who was also a leading member of the Order of St Lazarus. Coincidentally perhaps this order was the revived linear descendent of an Order of Lazarus that had been essentially a minor order of the Knights Templar.[4] This was not the only coincidence in this history.

The Black Knights

The other strange coincidence is that a number of those associated with early Freemasonry, particularly its earliest Jacobite form, were from families descended from people closely connected with the Knights Templar. This in a way should be expected, as rather than indicating a secret tradition of crypto-Templarism, it more likely simply demonstrates that certain aristocratic families were very interested in esoteric subjects and had often passed this interest on to some of their offspring. In the Middle Ages the Knights Templar had been a bolt hole for people with such interests, but in the 17th and 18th centuries Freemasonry was the preferred haven. Even the later in-law families of the notorious Masonic Sinclairs included men descended from Templar knights. This does not mean that Freemasonry shared any agenda with the Templars, in fact in many ways its later agenda was arguably diametrically opposed to a libertine aristocratic culture, and could be said to be the foundation of bourgeois society (particularly after the Protestant coup of 1717 which would shape Modern Freemasonry).3 It does mean however that individuals with access to certain traditions would have been present in both institutions. Thus while Freemasonry is certainly not a descendent of the Templars, this does not mean it has not inherited some of their knowledge and values via family connections. The Masons would not have had a monopoly of such traditions however, as some of the same families would have nothing to do with them and congregated in very different associations.

There is in fact one startling piece of evidence that seems to prove

The Black Knights

both a connection between Templar knowledge and Masonic secrets, as well as the later loss of this knowledge. That is the London Pentagram. I mentioned earlier the importance of the St Paul's ley in revealing a key Templar secret. But another feature of it reveals far more. It was observed that the St Paul's ley passes through the holy well of St Bride's church, though not the church itself. I long considered this a mystery, but on drawing a line through the church from apparent starting point of the St Paul's ley, a new alignment is formed. This alignment can actually be seen in Pilgrims Way, an old lane near St Pauls that exactly follows it, at the end of which the orientation of St Brides and St Pauls can be clearly seen. This alignment joins up with another of London's ley lines at the Marble Arch, near Tyburn or Speaker's Corner. Furthermore it became apparent that if two of London's oldest track ways, now Charing Cross Road and Oxford Street, were treated as ley lines, an irregular pentagram emerged from their orientation to this new alignment and two other traditional ley lines, the Strand ley and the London Stone ley. The corners of this pentagram being located at Ludgate Hill, Barbican Hill and at what is now Trafalgar Square, along with the Tyburn crosspoint and a unmarked locus in Bloombury. Moreover, key cross lines occurred at the significant site of St Clement Danes church and St Giles near what is now Centrepoint. But most surprising of all was the discovery that the exact centre of the pentagram lay at what is now the Connaught Rooms, but was once the Freemasons Tavern, the inn chosen by the first Freemasons as the centre of their London activity. The bisecting line of which passed southwards straight to the Outer

The Black Knights

Court of the Temple Inn, later used as a centre by the early Royal Society and now housing the Devereux Pub. Most oddly of all was that the site later chosen by Modern Freemasonry as it Grand Lodge Temple was not orientated to any of this, but stood out disconnected a hundred yards or more down the road. The fragmented history of the Freemasons had been ironically recorded in their architecture. All of this seems too much of a coincidence. The hidden implication is that this pentagram had in fact been formed by the position of St Bride's church. We know that Wren's church was built on the remains of the earlier church damaged in the Great Fire. We also know that this church dates to the late 12th century but that the site had been dedicated to St Bride for centuries before. But we don't know the site of the former religious buildings, despite claims to have found the foundations of previous churches beneath it. Archaeologists certainly found the remains of an ancient Roman dwelling beneath the church's foundations, but it was not a religious house, despite the area reputably being a religious site in late Roman times. I would therefore hazard a guess that the original sacred centre was nearer the well and the site of the current church was fixed later, perhaps as late as the 12th century, at the same time the Templar church was being constructed. Though an earlier date would make the mystery even more of an enigma. Perhaps indicating a project of Saxon stone masons rather than Templars.

The more certain fact of familial connections between the Templars and some Freemasons is also related to the idea that the Knights

The Black Knights

ST PAUL'S CATHEDRAL LEY, London

(diagram showing alignment: St Clement Danes — The Temple Church — St Bride's and Well — St Paul's Cathedral — St Helen's, Bishopsgate — St Dunstan's, Stepney, with North arrow)

The original St Paul's Ley of Watkins consisted of St Dunstan's, St Helen's, St Paul's and the Temple Church (4 degrees E of N) Devereux and Thompson altered the bearing fractionally and found St Clement Danes could be included as well. Neither St Bride's or its well was included, though recent groundwork indicates the original well probably lay on this line. If the line is modified by including St Bride's St Helen's and St Dunstans are lost but the Temple and St Clements just remain.

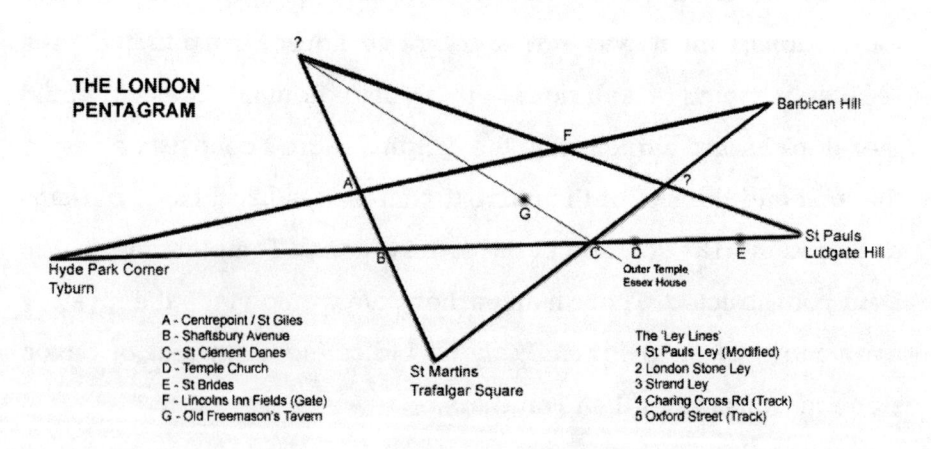

THE LONDON PENTAGRAM

(diagram of pentagram over London map)

- Barbican Hill
- St Pauls Ludgate Hill
- Hyde Park Corner / Tyburn
- Outer Temple / Essex House
- St Martins / Trafalgar Square

A - Centrepoint / St Giles
B - Shaftsbury Avenue
C - St Clement Danes
D - Temple Church
E - St Brides
F - Lincolns Inn Fields (Gate)
G - Old Freemason's Tavern

The 'Ley Lines'
1 St Pauls Ley (Modified)
2 London Stone Ley
3 Strand Ley
4 Charing Cross Rd (Track)
5 Oxford Street (Track)

124

The Black Knights

Templar were really run by those Black Knights of the higher aristocracy. And it is in tracing these that we may find some more clues, particularly in light of events during and after the Templars dissolution in England.

As already stated most of the Templar's property passed into the hands of the Knights Hospitaller, or the Order of St John. Including the Temple complex in London, which was first divided between the Inner Temple, initially in Royal hands and Hospitaller's Middle Temple, before the latter acquired both. Later still it was handed both over to the barristers of the Inns of Court, that still occupy it today. The Templar church is still run by a priest called the 'Master of the Temple' but his pedigree is strictly Hospitaller. This process was considerably more complex and drawn out than most people think. The King was extremely slow in handing over the Templars properties to the Hospitallers, giving many knights a long time to resettle elsewhere. In 1313 the Temple in London was initially siezed by the Crown, but put into the custody of none other than Aymer de Valence, the then Earl of Pembroke, our speculative real power behind the English Templars. This was challenged by the Earl of Lancaster who acquired the property the following year. But on his execution in 1322 it reverted to Pembroke who retained it till 1324. Meanwhile the Middle Temple and apparently certain precincts of the Templar church, had gradually been seeded to the Hospitallers, but in 1324 another Pembroke relative, Hugh Despenser, gained possession of most of the Inner Temple and held it another two years until 1326, when it reverted back directly

The Black Knights

to the Crown. During his time the first lawyers seem to have been moved into the precincts. It was not until 1338 that the Hospitallers took full control of the Temple and continued this process, twenty five years after the Templars dissolution.

A very important question that few ask is what happened to the Outer Temple, if there was an Inner and a Middle Temple? Well there lies an interesting fact. The Outer Temple did indeed exist and consisted of a part of the Temple that was handed over to another monastic order, who had already acquired the St Clement Danes church nearby. Amazingly that order was the Priory of the Holy Sepulchre, from whom the Templars had originally emerged and still remained closely allied to. Many Templars joined this order on their dissolution as they had the Order of Lazarus not far away. The Priory did not hold the Outer Temple for long but quickly passed it on to The Bishop of Exeter, who built Exeter House there, his London residence. This was not part of the Inns of Court and so lost the appellation of Outer Temple, becoming separated by the later wall and gate. But was still part of the original Templar complex. It may not be a coincidence that an apparently sizeable influx of Templars to Devon, if church records are anything to go by, began in the period that the Bishop was based here. In Elizabethan times Exeter House passed into the hands of Robert Dudley, the Earl of Leicester and was briefly renamed Leicester House. Before being passed on to his stepson Robert Devereux, the Earl of Essex and renamed Essex House. Frequent visitors to the house included members of the Sidney Circle and probably their mentor John Dee. From whom it gained a

The Black Knights

reputation as a centre of esoteric study. Later suspects in the Gunpowder Plot also met there. Today the Devereux pub stands on part of the site of this extensive house and grounds. As did its predecessor the Grecian Coffee House, in the Restoration period, becoming an early venue for the proto Masonic Royal Society.

Given this we can look a little closer at the 'Templar families'. As several authors have noted most of the Templar activity in England was on the Welsh Marches and neighbouring West Country, from where they were assisting the English King in his conquest of a rebellious Wales, as he saw it. It therefore should not be surprising that the two most powerful families who backed the Templars financially and socio-politically would be located here: the de Clares, as Earls of Gloucester and Pembroke; and their allies the Beaumonts, as Earls of Warwick and Leicester. These two twined houses would remain central to English occultism for generations, even though the familial inheritance of the title was discontinuous. An explicable puzzle, as there is evidence that when there was no direct kin connection in this lineage (such as via marriage and the maternal line), another of the allied families served as a medium of social transmission, that is they connected the familial phases of a house as a social bridge.[5] Closely allied to these two dynasties were their south-eastern kin the de Veres, the Earls of Oxford; their northern kindred the Percys, the Earls of Northumberland (who were closely related to the de Ros and Balliol families who among the earliest patrons of the Templars); and to some extent the Howards of East Anglia (descendents of the Mowbrays and Bigods,

The Black Knights

who inherited the role of Marshals of England after the Marshall Earls of Pembroke became extinct). Later the de Grey family, founders of that other Inn of Court, Greys Inn, would purposefully marry into all these families and become a central grapevine for the dynasties. The de Greys were apparently also heavily involved in Hermetica and witchcraft, though unlike the others they have no known links with the Knights Templar or their backers. This arguably further demonstrates we are dealing with a much broader tradition, of which the Templars were just one part at one moment of time. Although a highly significant part historically. Other significant families were the Stanleys, the Earls of Derby and Barons Strange, who were closely related to the Herbert Earls of Pembroke; as well as the Despensers, who linked the Pembrokes and the Warwicks through marriage. Many significant baronial families with magical interests married into this close dynastic web and then tend to continually intermarry with each other, forming an occult subculture, with perhaps adverse side effects over time. They also frequently sought royal marriages, sometimes successfully, in Order to enhance their power. This should not be interpreted as a vast extended family of course, as family rivalries continued to exist within this context. Perhaps a good analogy might be a kind of occult Mafia, which retained an overall culture and fundamental alliance, but consisted of several families and alliances which sometimes entered into competition and rivalry as power seekers are apt to. Much of this no doubt remains hidden, but occasionally broader schisms can be seen, as in sides taken in the War of the Roses; the religious schisms of the Catholicism of

The Black Knights

Mary vs the Anglican cult of the Virgin Queen and later of Catholic and Protestant; and the political schisms of Parliamentarian and Jacobite and Whig and Tory. All of which were complexly culturally entwined and had their esoteric elements and points of occult contention.

To put more flesh on these occult associations lets look at a few examples, though a full exploration would probably fill its own volume. We have already explored the de Clare and Beaumont origins in the William Rufus affair, as well as their association with the Marshal family, who succeeded the de Clares as Earls of Pembroke and briefly acquired the allied Earldom of Warwick, as well as being actively involved with the Templars. It is also well worth noting that the Warwicks appear to have maintained their role as the main English patron of the Priory of the Holy Sepulchre, right up until the dissolution of the Templars. The title was later inherited by the Dudley family, in the reign of Elizabeth I, as was the related Earldom of Leicester, which passed to Robert Dudley, the occult minded courtier, who was John Dee's primary backer. Later still the title passed on via a sister of Robert Devereux to the Rich family, who were in turn related to their London neighbours the Percys of Syon House, through another Devereux sister. It was in the Syon House of the early 17th century that the ninth 'Wizard' Earl of Northumberland, Henry Percy, was patron to the School of Night, a 'left hand path' Hermetic society, that the Richs of Holland House in Kensington were probably also a part.

This group merits a closer exploration for it was this society,

The Black Knights

founded by the alchemical Hermeticist and explorer Sir Walter Raleigh, the doyen of the Devonshire gentry, that Shakespeare appeared to mock in his Love Labours Lost. Without entering that esoteric labyrinth of the question of who Shakespeare 'really was' - with its colourful denizens, such as Hermeticist Francis Bacon of Grey's Inn [6] and the precocious de Vere heir of Oxford - it will suffice to observe the role played by the Herbert family, the then Earls of Pembroke, as patrons of the arts. Particularly the 3rd Earl, William Herbert, the main sponsor of Shakespeare, with the help of his relatives the Derbys, who later inherited the mantle of masters of the School of Night from Northumberland.

Shakespeare's sonnets, it should be remembered, also included a Romantic love cycle involving a 'poet' and a 'dark lady' whose love is sought but lost, reminiscent of the old Troubadour tales. Real life candidates for these characters include the Earl of Pembroke, William Herbert and his mistress Mary Fitton. Perhaps preserving a tradition of the Pembroke's, who were not only descendents of the Marshalls and de Clares, but also related to the Welsh Llewellyn clan, ancient sponsors of the Bardic tradition, whom the de Clares had married during their rooting in Wales. Earlier Mary Herbert, nee Mary Sidney, daughter of Henry Sidney and his wife, the sister of the Earl of Leicester, had married William Herbert's father and become Countess of Pembroke. As a disciple of her brother, Sir Philip Sidney, founder of the famous occult circle inspired by John Dee, she had been the patron of the esoteric poet Edmund Spencer and had also sponsored an alchemical laboratory at Wilton House, for Walter Raleigh's half brother and mentor Sir Humphrey Gilbert.

The Black Knights

Both of whom had served the Sidney family in Ireland, who were currently continuing the colonisation of that country, started by the de Clares and Marshals in County Clare. Such was the entangled nature of this familial grapevine.

The School of Night itself was a philosophically sceptical variant the Invisible College, with a similar Alchemical and Hermetic element. Their Saturnine trademark seems to have been a reverence for a 'dark lady', associated with night, if Shakespeare is a reliable witness, who probably represented a form of Sophia, the Gnostic 'goddess' of wisdom and revelation. This archetype appears to be one which harks back to the Black Madonna, Persephone and Mary of Egypt of the Templars. The group was also one of apparent political intrigue, with several members involved in plots both in favour of Stuart monarchs and against them, seemingly determined by whether their agenda was being championed or not. The height of which being the Gunpowder Plot of which Henry Percy was suspected of being the ringleader and imprisoned in the Tower for a number of years (while others claim this was simply a fit up of a dangerous conspirator). The School was also connected to Holland House in Kensington, via the Devereux link between the Rich family and Henry Percy, built on land formally owned by the de Veres, who also had their own Feylore here.[7] The evolving mythos being as tangled as the bloodlines it seems.

The de Veres themselves were often refered to as 'the stars' after their heraldic symbol of a five pointed star and the alleged high virtue of their character. We shall let history bare witness to that

The Black Knights

claim. But this appellation of 'star' tended to spread like a meme amongst the families, usually signifying an inspired poet or adept of somekind.

Another influential occult Order traceable to Devon and Somerset was the early 17th century Dragon Order, which is said to have numbered the Adams family amongst its members and seems to have been a kind of rural Hermetic, Neo-Druid Order, perhaps influenced by the likes of the local Stukeley family.[8] This group often chose pubs called the Green Dragon for its meetings, which, by now unsurprisingly, were named after the heraldic symbol of the locally influential Herbert family, the Earls of Pembroke. It may have also had some possible connection with the Pembroke's former agent and local hero Sir Walter Raleigh, known as 'El Draco' or 'the Dragon' by his Spanish enemies, who regarded him as a villain and arch conspirator.

The Dragon Order seems to have had somekind of relationship with another unnamed quasi-pagan network - linked by their old enemies the Puritans to the 'Satanic' Cult of Dagon. This was founded, it appears, by Fernando Gorges, governor of the English port of Plymouth, and later the American colony of Maine, and a close associate of both Walter Raleigh and Robert Devereux. This alleged 'Dagon society', to use the evocative Puritan name, appears to be associated with various Mermaid Taverns across England and had links with both independent seafaring and privateering. Both this network and the Dragons were associated

The Black Knights

with early colonies in the New World.

The Gorges network seems to have backed the famous 'ideal colony' at Merrymount (aka Mary or Mare Mount, based on it's founder's punning), or 'Mount Dagon' as the Puritans called it. This nautical coastal community had been founded by the decadent Royalist Thomas Morton, who attempted to integrate a libertine English 'folk culture', possibly even a dual faith paganism, with the shamanic ways of friendly indigenous tribes. The colony was ultimately destroyed by the then more influential Puritans, ostensibly for supporting Indian raiding parties against them. Its Maypole, cum totem pole, was symbolically hacked to the ground. Morton found support in exile at London's famous Mermaid Tavern, from Francis Bacon's secretary Ben Jonson and his circle who met there, and through influential friends was able to revoke the license given to the Puritan's main power base, the Massachusetts Bay Company. Ultimately alas on his return he was forced to seek sanctuary with his first backer Gorges, in Maine, as the well entrenched Puritans remained highly influential in New England. Other members of Merrymount community, somewhat suggestively, relocated to Salem and the Mount was redeveloped on more conventional lines by the wealthy Adams family. Alas we can only skim the surface of this fascinating secret history here,but it will suffice to say it was another mystery spawned by the families.

Returning to the Templars, it is an important fact, often ignored, that when King Edward reluctantly confiscated their property in the Inner Temple, in defiance of the Pope, who wanted it all handed to

The Black Knights

the Knights of St John, he installed one Hugh Despenser as his caretaker there. This family had not only married into the central de Clare, Beauchamp and de Vere families, but was also related to the St Armand family, from whom had earlier emerged one of the Masters of the Knights Templar. The Despenser family were also closely related to the influential Montacute or Montagu family. A family which later helped members of the Beauchamp and de Grey families form that Royalist cabal, the Order of the Garter, for Edward III (which many members of the other families subsequently joined, even the Gunpowder plotting 9th Earl of Northumberland!). They also later came into their own as one of the most prominent former Jacobite families to reconcile with the new order and carry some of the old esoteric traditions of the Ancient Freemasons back into the Modern Grand Lodge. Thus effectively creating the seeds of the first United Grand Lodge of England. Another member of this Masonic family also helped found the Bank of England. But perhaps most sensationally they were also the power behind the infamous Hell Fire Club, with its nominal founder Sir Francis Dashwood inheriting the Despenser title through marriage. Thus we have a common theme here involving familial networking and intermarriage, chivalric orders, the Jacobite rebellion, Freemasonry and banking, that constantly recurs in this history.

Not all the players in this history followed the Montagu path of course, many rebelled and emigrated to the Continent with their fellow hardcore Jacobites, while others choose a quieter and more comfortable life on the Celtic fringes of these Isles.

The Black Knights

The de Greys are another important family in this story, a dynasty with several branches, including one closely related to the Murray clan that became highly influential in Scottish Freemasonry. The later Earls Grey (of tea and politics fame) are thought by some to be the distant relatives of the same ancient family and certainly followed a similar agenda. The Greys had not been closely linked to the Templars, being descended from great churchmen and royal functionaries, though one of their ancestors denoted land around Hampton. They had come to the fore a little later and seem to have deliberately married into all the key families (or perhaps were cultivated by them, the instigators of marriages of this sort being uncertain). They also demonstrated a curious habit of marrying women later accused of witchcraft, or having strange magical powers.[9] Thus re-linking grassroots cults of witchcraft with their more noble counterparts and former 'Templar families'. Perhaps reaffirming the English Covenant and no doubt providing useful new blood to the dynasties.[10] One of the most famous of these noble witches allegedly being Elizabeth Woodville, a future Royal consort, whose family, like the early Plantagenets, claimed descent from the water fey Melusine - the legendary half human, half aquatic sprite, effectively a mermaid – and thus were often accused of witchcraft by their enemies. The most famous offspring to the de Grey – Woodville marriage was Lady Jane Grey, whose aristocratic supporters, including some those now familiar families then kin to the de Greys, sponsored her claim on the English throne. After this failed attempt rumours were unsurprisingly circulated about Lady Jane's occult practises. The aristocratic de Grey family, like many

The Black Knights

in this history, gradually died out as a influential dynasty, but their alleged relatives the Parliamentarian Earls Grey continued to be associated with both politics and esoteric activities. One link to them being the Fox family, both their political allies and kin to their relatives in the Rich family, who had inherited Holland House from them and still allegedly held strange rituals there.[11] This alliance was highly active in Whig politics. Finally the Grey family married into one of the richest of the rising new banking dynasties, the powerful Barings family and was absorbed into yet another new order. In time such banking families would become the new aristocracy.

Meanwhile, the Continental branches of the Templars had found their own separate modes of survival. Most prominently in Portugal, Northern Italy and to some extent within the Teutonic Knights, or even the English Order of St John with its overseas contacts.[12] As we shall see they also possibly survived in Switzerland. In Portugal the Order reverted back to the old name of the Knights of Christ and many Portugese and Spanish Templars joined this 'new' body. Unlike the Order of Montessa which was formed to inherit Templar property in Spain but retained few actual Templars. Originally Portugal had been created as a separate kingdom in Andalusia, effectively by the activity of the Knights Templar and was perhaps once thought of as a potential Ordensland by them. It seems however that the Knights of Christ were extensively reformed and driven back to orthodoxy by its later leaders, with some of its members, including Christopher

The Black Knights

Columbus, known for their messianic Christian fanaticism.

A purer strain may have survived in Florence, that influential Renaissance centre, where Dante Alighieri claimed to have been initiated into a secret post Templar Order, the mysterious Feda Santa and to have loosely based his epic chthonic quest, the Inferno, on its mysteries. Given what we have discovered of the Knights Templar's subterranean preoccupations this sounds quite plausible. Dante seems to have thought that by descending deep into 'hell' or 'sin', without falling prey to it, one could find an inverted path back to 'heaven' and beyond, much like the Nigredo phase of Alchemy. Prefiguring a dangerous path in modern occultism with many psychotic casualties. A safer variant of this philosophy was developed in England by the visionary artist William Blake, who was both a great follower and critic of Dante. Of course Dante was also greatly influenced by the Fedeli d'Amore group, who had preserved Troubadour lore and had influenced their most famous member Boccacio, in his erotic masterpiece, the Decameron, as well as the Islamic texts, the Night Voyage and the Book of the Ladder and the Papist society the Guelphs, who retained a more orthodox Catholic mysticism.

Both Florence and Portugal would become the favourite ports of call on the 'Grand Tours' of the English aristocracy, including many of those families we have been exploring here and ideas and images were inevitably brought home with them. Most famously in the popular Florentine classicism of the likes of the aforementioned

The Black Knights

Sir Francis Dashwood, a close friend of exiled Jacobites there and in Rome, who himself had inherited the Despenser barony, after marrying into the wealthy Fane family. From 1746 till 1780 Dashwood would continue and extend the Jacobite tradition of the 'Hell Fire Club'. An idea which also drew on the libertine philosophy of Rabelais - born in the wild Bacchanalian vineyards of Chinon and the fictional French Abbey of Theleme - who coined the phrase 'Do what thou wilt'. Dashwood had also been a senior member of the Druid Universal Bond, found in 1717 according to its legends, before being expelled for his Hell Fire Club activities. William Blake also briefly joined this society a generation later and may have picked up a few ideas here. Members of Francis Dashwood's club, that met deep in the caves beneath West Wycombe's church, included its joint founder the Earl of Sandwich, aka John Montagu (whose kinswoman Lady Montagu, the former lover of the Duke of Wharton, founder of the original Jacobite Hell Fire Club, allegedly presided over the club's orgies). Also members were the Secretary of State, the Earl of Bute, a close relative of the Montagus and of the Grey linked Murray clan; the Prince of Wales; the son of the Archbishop of Canterbury; John Wilkes MP, the radical English agent of Samuel Adam's Sons of Liberty and perhaps even Benjamin Franklin. Wilkes claimed they were secretly dedicated to Bona Dea, whose festival like Mary of Egypt was on 3rd April. While Dashwood himself lovingly decorated several of his classical architectural projects with images from the cults of Aphrodite and Dionysos (perhaps influenced by his father's important role in the Vintner's Guild and Anglo-French

The Black Knights

wine trade!) and hung the motto of Rabelais and the Hell Fire Club clearly above the entrance to their cavernous underworld.

Clearly this post Jacobite period was a time when the tradition was again becoming internationalised. The seeds of which had been sown since the Renaissance, with first exchanges of the Hermetic ideas and practitioners, that would greatly transform esoteric communities across Europe. The emergence of the Grand Tour in the Elizabethan and Jacobean period and the great exile of the Jacobites, brought this to a head and things were further consolidated by the emergence of certain sections of international Freemasonry. But deep at the heart of this was a reconnection of far older European traditions, traditions that had been protected by the Templars and modified by them to a certain extent. Since the destruction of the Order these old Templar traditions, largely preserved independently within various European families, had since seeded local forms of esotericism and secular practise. These were both original and rooted in the culture the Templars had helped propagate. It was these forms that were linking up and finding deep resonances within the newer Hermetic subculture. Of course this also included a strong political dimension as ever. With perhaps the most significant development being hinted at in Wilkes' later accusations, that members of the Hell Fire Club were scheming over the future of the rebel American colonies.

Perhaps another influential, international 'post Templarism' had earlier emerged in Switzerland. It has recently been suggested that the independence of the Swiss cantons and their confederation was

The Black Knights

achieved with the military assistance and patronage of the last of the Continental Knights Templar. Certainly the Swiss managed to employ some very well equipped mercenaries between the time of the Templar's demise in 1312 and the rebellion of the cantons against the Holy Roman Empire. Politically this decentralised, multicultural and democratic nature of Swiss society, together with its tacit social conformity, technological innovation and economic hierarchy, was just the sort of thing most Templars and their backers, would have wanted. There is also the issue of whether the Templars retained any of their wealth and if so where did it go. All the signposts here seem to point to Switzerland. This thesis is developed with some skill in the book the Warriors and the Bankers, by Butler and Defoe. It was also here that international banking was perfected, providing a basic economic foundation for other evolving banks, such as those of London and Northern Italy. Its close links to economic interests in France and Germany are also obvious. It could be thus argued that International Capitalism was thus to a certain extent a Templar invention.

More significantly we can see the innevitable schizoid split in all of this, with on the one hand a current emerging from the very roots of Templarism, for liberty, democratic equality and social unity and on the other a later perverse current of power seeking. The latter linked to elitism, wealth and social manipulation, which rises and dominates the culture. The tension between these irreconcilable opposites is a central feature of the evolution of this secret history in its later years. The many networks that have emerged from it have often been riven by this tension. But while certain individuals

The Black Knights

and small groups have made a stand for one current or the other, no true schism has yet emerged in the broader culture, which still writhes under the influence of these overlapping and conflicting currents.

It is obvious from these brief studies that at least some of the traditions of the Templars were handed down through certain branches of the families who had sponsored them. Before we conclude our study it is worth looking at what may be the most recent evolution of the tradition we have been exploring, as well as its most radical to date.

The ancient Oxbridge institution of Trinity College, Cambridge, like its peers Clare College and Pembroke College, was one of the many educational establishments founded by these families. Known as the aristocrat's college since Tudor times and still one of the largest landowners in Britain, in the past it was an important place of early networking and recruitment for a variety of elitist groups. Not only were members of the various families often educated here, but also their later allies, Francis Bacon and Isaac Newton being just two famous examples. But it is in more recent history that something particularly interesting occurred here.

Towards the end of the nineteenth century members of the Grey family and their kin appear predominantly on the rolls of the college, with at the turn of the century a member of the Herbert family, Lord Carnarvon, being a star student. Later he would become famous for financing the opening of the tomb of

The Black Knights

Tutankhamun and becoming the sole victim of its curse. Victorian Egyptianism was all the rage then, though Carnarvon doesn't seem to have been too interested himself, or to have had any occult interests, until sent to Egypt on health reasons and assigned the role. Curiously the man behind this was Lord Cromer, a member of the Baring family, who was indeed rumoured to have occult leanings. Perhaps indicating familial affiliations are as much to do with connections and trust as they are any 'secret traditions'.

But with regard to secret traditions another aspect of this story is highly interesting. For soon after Carnarvon left Trinity College another student arrived, one Aleister Crowley. Later Crowley and Carnarvon would be in Cairo at the same time and their paths would curiously converge on the growing Egyptianist fashion. But what Crowley brought into the world had deeper resonances with some of the far older traditions we have been exploring than many realise. A full analysis of these still needs to be undertaken, but it will suffice for now to list some of the curious parallels between what has been identified here as the inner 'Templar tradition' and what Crowley claimed to have achieved in trance.

The most obvious parallel is the phrase 'Do what thou will' and its connection with the splendid profanities of the libertine Abbey of Thelema. But there is far more here than just a rehash of Rabelais or Dashwood's Hell Fire Club. Apart from the obviously unique Gnosis in Crowley, as symbolically expressed within the Theosophised Hermeticism of his subculture, and the fashionably Egyptianised context it was couched in, there are many interesting points of contact between Thelema and the Templar tradition. The

The Black Knights

most central are the erotic aspects of Thelema, found not only in the Randolphian OTO [1] he made contact with, and the Hell Fire Club he at least read of, but arguably also in the very essence of the medieval Love Cult that had inspired the real founders of the Templars. As well as perhaps in the Fey marriage lore found in traditions on de Vere lands, which may have partly been the origin of the eighth degree of the OTO It is also worth repeating in this respect that the de Vere's heraldic symbol was a five pointed star and that they were sometimes referred to as the 'stars', the renowned 'starry de Vere' being a famous late example of this (we might also include in this Phillip Sidney's reference to Penelope Devereux as 'the star', or Stella, in his famous poem Stella and Astrophel, who briefly lived on the former de Vere estate at Kensington). As we have seen, this term for an adept also spread like a meme through the families we have been exploring. This apparently elitist appellation was wisely universalised by Crowley to all Mankind. Another obvious connection is Nuit, the central feminine principle in Crowley's Thelemic theology, a darker manifestation of an ancient Egyptian goddess, whose name means Night, and thus reminiscent of the School of Night and its dark patron of that name. The admirable, sceptically scientific orientation of this school also shines through in Crowley's writing, as does its emphasis on poetry. The Horus factor is more unique to Crowley, but the idea of these male and female divine figures is very familiar, being found as far back as the Sol Invictus cult, amongst the inner elite of the Hell Fire Club, and more recently in the Masonic Neopaganism of Wicca. This is particularly evident

The Black Knights

given Crowley's interest in these groups, and his constant identification of Horus with Baal, Dionysos and Pan. Moreover, Babalon, the immanent aspect of Nuit, is also basically Ishtar or Astarte, further fitting the pattern of the centrality of Astarte, that we have constantly found within the Tradition. And finally the idea of following ones 'True Will' is not unlike the Sufi notion of surrender to the 'Will of God', or the Nordic notion of Villi, or Will, seemingly identified with the Nordic Tyr, the St Nicholas of the Templars and Varangians. There is more here than a poetic vision or a piss take on Augustine!

Were it not for Crowley's connections this might be seen as a coincidental recombination of past material. But not only did he overlap both geographically and temporally with Carnarvon and other Trinity alumni, he had even closer relations with one of the Pembroke's more distant relatives and one whose occult interests were well known, Evan Morgan. Viscount Tredegar, was a well known eccentric in the 1930s, but less well known was his occult practice, but it was the latter which attracted Crowley, who called his friend the 'adept of adepts' and mysteriously 'the most fitting to wield Excalibur'. The latter perhaps being due to the Morgan family's ancient descent from the Llewellyns, who claimed Arthurian ancestry, as part of their tradition of Bardic patronage. As we have seen this family also intermarried with the Pembroke de Clares at an early date, bringing them into the orbit of our Black Knights. So the Morgans too fall into this lineage, perhaps one of the last in a long line of such families. However Crowley's 1930s association with Morgan was too late for it to have had much of an

The Black Knights

influence on the formation of Thelema. But one person who did have a big early influence on him was MacGregor Mathers his first mentor. This Neo-Jacobite magus was himself a long time friend of the heiress Lady Caithness, the doyen of the Parisian occult scene. This wealthy esotericist had not only helped form the Theosophical Society - Madame Blavatsky being once in her employ as a trance medium - but had also organised the famous séances that led to the formation of Doinel's Neo-Gnostic Church. And interestingly she herself was one of the last mystics in the Scottish nobility, albeit through marriage. Her inlaws included the Sinclairs, Butes and Murrays and so was another well placed person within the tradition to have influenced Mathers and through him Crowley himself.

Interestingly one of the first people Mathers contacted in London, when the Hermetic Order of the Golden Dawn was founded, was Rose Cross Mason Wynn Westcott, a descendent of the St Leger Templars. The 'Great Beast' later fell out with Mathers and cast him as the evil sorcerer in his novel Moonchild, curiously he casts himself as heroic magician, under the name of Grey! Perhaps this is really all coincidence, or due to Crowley's skill at unearthing secrets, scholarly or psychically, but I think these connections are very suggestive.

Crowley never had a monopoly on unearthing secret traditions, even if his take on it is in part a particularly aesthetic one. Other modern occult group have also acquired or reconstructed such knowledge from other sources. Even individualists like Austin Osman Spare seems to echo the tradition of the same dark goddess

The Black Knights

in the trend for atavistic magic. Which in many ways is an intensification of the current. By the end of the 20th century the tradition had spread wide, became far more egalitarian and diversified greatly.

1. The original Neo-Gnostic Church, from which all the primary Gnostic Churches of today are descended, was formed from a fusion of three strands, the late 19th century Neo-Gnostic Church of Father Doinel, formed from a combination of scholarly research, Theosophical mediumship and outright forgery; the notorious 'Satanic' Gnostic Church of Carmel, basically a 19th century Hermetic sex cult; and Fabre-Palaprat's earlier Templarist Johannite Church, which supplied a foundation for their union. This house of cards was later reinforced by some equally controversial Apostolic successions acquired illegitimately from Eastern Churches. The original OTO, formed within the fringe Masonic Order of Memphis and Misraim - which had absorbed many occult currents, especially the sex magic innovations of P B Randolph, was particularly influenced by one offshoot of this Neo-Gnostic Church working with westernised Tantra.

2. This assumption follows the likely scenario that Modern Freemasonry represents a middle class hijacking of an aristocratic tradition. Evidence, although sparse, indicates that as the rising Protestant middle class entered the elite Masonry of the largely Catholic aristocracy they were kept within the three degrees of Craft Masonry, and not allowed to pass the veil into the higher degrees, which were constantly being invented to distance them. Following the Protestant Revolution however these higher degrees were effectively cut off and a new Grand Lodge invented to foster a Craft Masonry of three degrees. This also cut Craft Masonry off from much of its occult roots. However it was not long before the higher degrees reasserted themselves in a new form.

3. The claim that the French Revolution was a conspiracy is a ludicrous assertion generally put forward by right wing reactionaries. The Revolution was of course a popular uprising shaped by complex historical factors. However amongst these complex factors was the known conspiratorial activity of a variety of covert groups with diverse agendas, which occasionally influenced key events. The most influential faction of these was led by the Duc d'Orleans from the Palais Royal, who desired a reformed, liberal monarchy with a proto-socialist agenda. But perhaps the most famous was the allied remnant of the Bavarian Illuminati, then working through its French initiate Nicholas de Bonneville, which desired a far more radical left wing agenda. Both of these groups used the popular myth of the Templars in what today we might

The Black Knights

call psychological warfare (one further radicalised later by the anarchist artist Rossetti). For more see Billington's Fire in the Minds of Men. An area of further interest is the support given to d'Orleans' ancestor during his exile in Britain in the mid 19th century, by members of English Masonry allied to the Whig party.

4. The Order of Lazarus was originally a monastic hospital for lepers, which under the influence of the Knights Templar became an order of leper and non-leper knights, mostly constituted by infected Templars. The rationale behind this was that in an early stage of their illness a leper was not only infectious but had a dead nervous system, which meant they could not feel pain or even suffer at the loss of a limb. This combined with the typical disfigurement of the leper made them a fearsome unit of shock troops. The Order of St Lazarus in London was based at the current site of Lincoln's Inn Fields off Chancery Lane, which had also been a training ground for the Templars. Even after the last leper member of the Order had died and its members perfectly healthy, many feared to enter its doors graced as they were with the stone effigies of deformed lepers. The chivalric order that descended from it was a purely honorific body, though it is often claimed that after the dissolution of the Templars many knights sought refuge in the ranks of its predecessor.

5. As the Devereux family - themselves descended from close kin of the House of Pembroke (Hastings) - did for the Dudleys and Richs in the House of Warwick and the de Greys had for the Dudleys and Beauchamps, the latter themselves direct descendents of the Beaumonts.

6. Grey's Inn, like the other Inns in the late 16th century, was not just a school of barristers, but a general college for the aristocracy, which also had a licentious reputation. Francis Bacon is said to have helped form a secret society here, variously known as the Order of the Helmet, the Knights of Athena. This group sponsored the arts and may have also been linked to Bacon's proposal for an Invisible College, like that of the Rosicrucians soon to seek exile in Britain and join his cause. Some have even argued 'Shakespeare' was a name applied to this collective, which also included several other candidates, such as de Vere, Marlowe and Ben Jonson. This group was also linked to the Arcadian Areopagus, often represented simply by the letters AA, which appeared to decorate the groups publications (which may have also punned on various combinations of the group's mythic patrons, Athena, Apollo, Adonis and Aphrodite as well as having symbolic significance). This AA were either a broader manifestation of Bacon's activities, or were a network originally founded by Phillip Sidney, with the assistance of the Countess of Pembroke. The ubiquitous appearance of the boar in Bacon's works, ostensibly a pun on his name may also have indicated some unknown connection with the de Vere family, whose heraldry included the totemic Blue Boar. Rumours that Bacon was the illegitimate son of the Earl

The Black Knights

of Leicester and Queen Elizabeth remain controversial. Suggestively Grey's Inn was named after its first owner the medieval Lord Grey.

7. The de Vere's in England were founded by Auberon de Vere, whose name inspired Oberon as the King of the Fey, first used in England by William Shakespeare. The name Auberon was itself derived from Alberich, or Elf King, originally the legendary supernatural half brother of Merovee, the founder of the Merovingian dynasty, whom the Flemish inlaws of the de Veres believed themselves descended from. The de Vere estate of Holland Park in Kennsington was the site of the legend of Kenna – local Queen of the Fey and daughter of Oberon and Titania of nearby Kensington Gardens – who had eloped with the human King Albion, starting an apocalyptic war and after whom the area was named. The legend contains subtle hints of changeling hybridisation and the 'marriage' of mortals and elementals.

8. According to Andrew Rothovius, the Dragons were an occult group much interested in megaliths and geomancy, as were many in the West Country and greatly influenced by Arthurian and Grail mythology, who politically first supported a branch of the Stuart family and when in exile became champions of the American Revolution. It is also possible they had an earlier origin in Elizabethan England, perhaps under Raleigh. In America they are linked to the rebel Samuel Adams, whose Masonic 'Sons of Liberty' group met in a lodge at the Green Dragon Tavern in Boston (that Pembroke related inn, curiously founded by a member of the Perkins family, earlier mentioned in relation to the English Covenant, and later bearing one of the Salem witches!). The Order of the Dragon should not be confused with Gardiner's probably fictitious and extreme right wing Imperial Dragon Court.

9. Another aristocratic 'witch' the de Grey family married was Antigone, the daughter of the wizard Duke of Gloucester and the sorceress Eleanor Cobham. Earlier they had married another member of the Cobham family and later took one Catherine Strangeways into their family. All of whom had reported links to local witches. In the case of Eleanor Cobham this led to the execution of her accomplice, Margery Jourdemayne, the 'witch of Eye'. This tendency to marry witches can be seen as a family of occult minded aristocrats trying to improve their magical position, or more speculatively could have been an attempt to consolidate magical 'bloodlines', whether understood as archaic fey lore, or today in terms of a recessive 'psychic gene'.

10. We often find the heirs of these families in later years marrying the descendents of Templar patrons, such as the Greys, or more significantly descendents of former Templar Masters, such as the Hastings, the St Legers and the Baskervilles as well as former vassals.

The Black Knights

11. The Fox family were a very unusual bunch, supporters of radical liberalism (and at one time of Napoleon and the French Revolution), who organised garden parties, masked balls and artistic soirees at Holland House (which included guests as diverse as Charles Dickens, Wordsworth and Lord Byron), they also appear to have marked the death of Charles I by draping the house in black every January 30th, while engaging in a day long fast and a mysterious ceremony. The proximity of this day to Candlemass or Imbolc is not lost on Neo-Pagans, who might understandably regard this as a dark night before dawn. The founder of the family Stephen Fox had been a member of a secret society that helped restore Charles II to the throne in the mid 17th Century, having been recruited by Henry Percy. The Wizard Earl's involvement and the later Holland House acquisition, suggests it is also possible that this activity was related to the School of Night (Jan 30th was also the execution date of the Gunpowder Plotters!). Charles James Fox MP, a later member of the family became an influential Whig politician and almost Prime Minister in 1784. He was assisted in this campaign by Georgiana (nee Spencer) Cavendish, the Duchess of Devonshire, a libertine political activist and proto feminist, who was the mistress of Charles Grey, the 2nd Earl Grey. She herself was also an heir of the Despenser line. Curiously a Continental occultist had claimed that she was regarded by some occultists in England as the reincarnation of Mary Magdeline, only to be quickly corrected and suppressed by his English brethren. Her manner of securing votes for Fox was said to be highly personal.

12. The English Order of St John remained part of an international association for many centuries after the Crusades. Interestingly in England members of the de Vere family had also become the priors of the Order of St John and family allies retained some limited influence within the English branch of the Hospitallers for many years after. The Order of course later broke away as an independent body from its Continental brothers who mostly retained their Papal loyalty. Today the Knights of Malta maintain its heritage in Rome.

The Black Knights

The Black Knights

Conclusion

What can we conclude then about the Knights Templar? I would argue the evidence, including that of the Chinon document, strongly indicates they were primarily a military order of diverse constitution. Their members being selected for their loyalty and dedication to the Order, as they percieved it, rather than for their beliefs. Most of the Templar knights were uneducated and many no doubt quite orthodox in whatever superstitious beliefs they may have held, particularly in the last years of the Order. Some originally joined to escape situations in Europe, using the Order as a kind of foreign legion and rehab centre. On the other hand, few, notably its lawyers, diplomats and bankers, were in contrast relatively well educated however and usually dominated the Grandmaster's council. This group served the Order's real agenda in the covert service of the traditional feudal aristocracy.

The Black Knights

This educated apex of the Order was in close contact with those I argue were the real heads of the Templars, the barons who financed them in exchange for their use as a private army, bank and personal Church. An army technically that of a distant Pope, but in reality under the power of those local nobles who sponsored them. Whose influence was no doubt mediated by those Black Knights who joined the various secular Templar confraternities and obtained and distributed Templar privileges. Secular members who gained the right to sit on and no doubt dominate, the Grand Master's and provincial Master's councils. Whose influence was further enhanced in later years, when such layman were also allowed to become Preceptors or Commanders of local Templar Houses, if no monastic candidate was available.

As an institution the Templars were relatively tolerant for their age, promoting the concept of respect and private belief. Probably to create a culture in which their own private beliefs would be tolerated. For within the original Order many were genuinely heretical in the eyes of the Church, smething also making their exemption from excommuncation essential. Later of course when they became a powerful institution, officially loyal to the Pope, the majority of their rank and file would be far more orthodox and as such distanced from the Templars foundations.

That said however, I argue there does seem to have always been an 'inner unorthodoxy' within the Templars. Both within the higher ranks of the Order, who were allowed to progress, and amongst its most enthusiastic patrons. Originally rooted in a Troubadour culture of the Divine Feminine, emerging from Moorish Spain and

The Black Knights

further taking on various Ismailian and Sufi elements in Palestine. With apparently one later faction taking this to a greater degree, and probably introducing heretical rites, such as those involving Nazari like doctrines and their denial of faith.

This increasingly became an elite sectarianism within the Templar Order however, with the bulk of the institution more orthodox. Thus the beliefs and politics of the Templars as a whole were those of their local patrons, be they idiosyncratic Catholics, moderate Cathars, of dual faith, or even Sabbatic witches! Their only code seems to have been one of aristocratic sovereignty, privileged liberty, mutual loyalty and local tradition. With at their best a paternalistic attitude to their serfs, and at worst an exploititive elitism. With perhaps the traditional inner sect barely holding sway between the factions.

Another aspect that should be highlighted here is that the tradition of enoblement and paternalism also included a certain commitment to both education and the arts. In its earliest form this was part of the Bardic tradition that came under the protection of certain families. Later it formed a more general attachment to the arts and poetry in particular, reaching its apex with the patronage of Shakespeare but continueing long after. This in turn could take the form of either a status symbol, as could works of charity, or in some cases a genuine attempt at cultural enhancement. The same pattern can be found today within both corporate sponsorship and fringe counterculture. Both in their own way Templar heritages.

The Black Knights

Originally beneath this uniquely 'Templar' phenomenon there appears to have been a traditional dual faith belief system, probably quite common at the time. A part Christian, part Pagan religion, that revered the Saints and their relics in terms of pagan folk myth. In the Templar's case this included John the Baptist, St Nicholas, St Lawrence and St George, and in addition to the Virgin Mary, particularly popular female saints, principally the Magdalene, Mary of Egypt and St Catherine, all of whom being anciently rooted in Persephone, Consort of Hades. While in Normandy and England, at least for some, this seems to have bordered on a purer Celto-Nordic paganism, disquised only by a thin veneer of surface Christianity. With the Anglo-Normans faction unique in creating a stratified Covenant, which at its beginning extended down to a loyal, grassroots crypto-paganism, and even perhaps a hidden subculture of 'witchcraft'.

This English Covenant outlasted the Templars, whose ideas and practises were largely absorbed into it, and appears to have been something of a family affair at every level. Over time however its vertical components were seperated by increasingly obvious social divisions in Europe and the decline of the 'organic society" that supported it. While on the horizontal level, violent family feuds increasingly fragmented the network, with individual benefit increasingly overiding traditional communal values. For the aristocracy culminating in the War of the Roses and the Civil Wars of the Reformation that decimated the traditional nobility and eradicated much of the higher teachings. Eventually its remnants became the grapevine of fringe cults that made up the English

The Black Knights

Mystery Tradition.

The actual rituals carried out by the Templars would have included dubbing, if not already a knight; an initiation in a chapel, involving vow taking and monastic ordination if appropriate; a communion mass (in which the sacraments were sometimes alleged to be profane or missing); and at least some form of secret cryptic or subterranean initiation. The latter is unknown and was probably reserved for higher ranking or selected members. From the little info we have it probably involved death rituals, both in general terms of a Mass for the Dead, the origin of the Black Mass, and specific initiation rites, probably very similar to the Masters, and even to the Royal Arch and Cryptic Degrees of Freemasonry. These may have been in fact based on Templar degrees, if the early Jacobite Masons who invented them were drawing on recorded family traditions. Some of these rites involved a blindfolded candidate passing through veils and facing elemental ordeals, perhaps originally like the Knighten Guild's, before entering a dark cavern beneath the Temple Mount, where they face death before being reborn. The latter setting now doubt modelled on the Well of Souls beneath the Temple, and recreated in the various caves and crypts used by the Templars all over the world. There was of course also the denial ritual, which was either a test of faith or more likely an entrance into a secret order within the Templars. Though arguably this was later and limited in application

But the real esoteric activity of the Templars was carried out

The Black Knights

amongst those Black Knights who were the real force behind the Order and it was in their families that these traditions survived long after the demise of the Knights. Traditions that were later partly inherited and reused by other arcane groups, as diverse as the Freemasons, the Rosicrucians, Illuminati and the various other Hermetic brotherhoods. Some of their knowledge was also said to have been acquired by witch families and certain tribes of Romany gypsies, who traversed the roads guarded by the knights and sometimes served them, but all this is hard to verify.

Most importantly it should not be mistakenly thought that some complete body of 'Templar knowledge' was ever passed on wholemeal. For one there probably never was such a thing, given the Templars natural idiosyncrasies. But also each generation will naturally reinterpret what it receives and adds new material from other sources. One big change in the received tradition within the English Covenant no doubt occurred during the Renaissance with its influx of Hermetic material. What remains constant is a subcultural tradition and a basic model.

But the broader cultural legacy of the Order was twofold and highly ambivalent. On one hand they were the first Capitalists, whose drive for power created the first international bank and global corporation, the prototype of those we now suffer. While on the other hand they were the first rebellious libertarians, individuals eager to empower themselves and those they regarded as their peers. These two currents, initially regarded as compatible, outlived the Knights Templar and have had a major impact on

The Black Knights

modern society. Though initially entwined in their emergent forms these trends would later naturally begin to come apart and conflict with each other. This would be an important feature of the tradition's later development.

Today the secular heirs of the Templar bankers again support wars of imperial conquest in the Middle East. Again often working covertly through private Christian armies, such as Blackwater, manned by ex-military personnel and dubious mercenaries just like the Templars had been. Both were private security forces which aimed to become rich from war and become a political force in their own right through this wealth. But this is a perverted repetition of the Templars in many ways, though in this case motivated more by greed and control, than by liberation and personal empowerment. Likewise State and private intelligence agencies, their client states and their co-opted terrorist organisations, act much like the mercenaries and Assassins of old. Though again as a tragic perversion of these ancient orders. Whose purpose is now to create, through fear and anxiety, repressive security states within a 'new world order'. An agenda that would have been beloved by the Cluniacs perhaps, but hated by genuine Templars. Fortunately at the same time the last streams of those esoteric and radical currents safeguarded by the Knights Templar continue to universalise and democratise. Preserving and evolving the tradition of spiritual liberty for the 21st Century.

Seven hundred years on the Knights Templar may have vanished

The Black Knights

into the mists of time and their heirs fragmented but their spirit lives on for good and ill.

Every Man and Every Woman is a Star.

1. The Wars of the Roses was a turning point in the history. Arising from a local feud between the traditionalist Percy family and the ever more avaricious Neville dynasty, it drew in more and more of the Templar families on both sides and eventually split the Royal Family. The decimation that resulted was aptly summed up by Shakespeare in Henry VI where after the sides tellingly pick their symbolic roses from Garden of the Middle Temple, he has Warwick say:

'And here I prophesy: this brawl to-day, Grown to this faction in the Temple-garden, Shall send between the red rose and the white, A thousand souls to death and deadly night'.

The Black Knights

SELECT BIBLIOGRAPHY

M Baigent, R Leigh, H Lincoln, *The Holy Blood and the Holy Grail* (Cape 1982)

Malcolm Barber, *The Trial of the Templars* (CUP 1978)

Malcolm Barber, *The New Knighthood* (CUP 1994)

David V Barrett, *Secret Societies* (Cassell 2007)

W B Bartlett, *The Assassins* (Sutton 2001)

Ean Begg, *The Cult of the Black Virgin* (Arkana 1997)

James Billington, *Fire in the Minds of Men* (New York 1980)

Muriel Bradbrook, *The School of Night* (1936)

Alan Butler & Stephen Defoe, *The Warriors and the Bankers* (Templar Books 1998)

Aleister Crowley, *The Book of the Law* (Mandrake 1992)

John Charpentier, *L'Ordre des Templiers* (Paris 1962)

John Constable, *The Southwark Mysteries* (Oberon Books 2000)

J Koehnline & R Sakolsky, *Gone to Croatan* (Autonomedia/AK 1994)

Evelyn Lord, *The Knights Templar in Britain* (Longman 2004)

Walter Map, *Master Walter Map's Book* (London 1924)

Sean Martin, *The Knights Templars* (Pocket Essentials 2004)

Lynn Picknett and Clive Prince, *Templar Revelation* (Bantam 1997)

Helen Nicholson, *The Knights Templar* (Sutton 2001)

Peter Partner, *The Murdered Magicians* (OUP 1981)

James Sharpe, *Instruments of Darkness* (Hamish Hamilton 1996)

Eric Towers, *Dashwood : The Man and Myth* (Crucible 1986)

James Wasserman, *The Templars and the Assassins* (Destiny 2001)

Frances Yates, The *Occult Philosophy in the Elizabethan Age*, (Routledge 1979)

The Black Knights

Stephen J Ash is a London based writer / researcher and philosopher. He has been studying the Knights Templar and related subjects, for the past fifteen years and has a life long experience of various esoteric matters. He also writes on philosophy, science, art and cultural issues and is well known in specialist circles for his left libertarian writings, as well as his articles in Oracle Magazine. In 2002 he graduated from Kings College London with a Masters Degree in Philosophy and History of Science and has since worked as a freelance speaker / tutor. He also develops and runs alternative tours of London. His current writing projects include the Garden of the Temple, a complete genealogy of the English Covenant families and a detailed exploration of the mythos.

The Black Knights

The Black Knights